Science K-1: Earth Science

Schola Rosa Cycle 2

by

Alecia J. Rolling, M.A.

Charisma DaSilva, M.S.

Cover Image Credit: Public Domain Image provided by Amazon Kindle Direct Publishing.

Image Credits: All images in this book have been created by Charisma DaSilva unless otherwise noted with the image, such credited images being in the public domain.

ISBN: 9798669441685

Independently Published.

TABLE OF CONTENTS

Introduction	1
Unit 1	3
Unit 2	11
Unit 3	19
Unit 4	25
Unit 5	31
Unit 6	39
Unit 7	45
Unit 8	51
Unit 9	59
Unit 10	67
Unit 11	75
Unit 12	83
Unit 13	89
Unit 14	97
Unit 15	101
Unit 16	103
Unit 17	111
Unit 18	123
Unit 19	133
Unit 20	147
Unit 21	159
Unit 22	171
Unit 23	179
Unit 24	187
Unit 25	199
Unit 26	217
Unit 27	229
Unit 28	239
Unit 29	245
Unit 30	257

Introduction to Science

Welcome! To help you make use of the lessons and activities throughout the cycle a few notes of explanation and direction are necessary here at the beginning. These notes also provide a general overview of the 3-year cycle of Science provided with the *Schola Rosa Home Curriculum.*

Goals. There are four general goals for the Science program:

1. To bring the children into contact with the physical world in enriched experiential encounters
2. To practice and improve careful observation; a basic tool of learning and an essential first step in all education, including that accomplished by use of the scientific method
3. To introduce (in 4–6th grades) the basic paradigm of the scientific method
4. To introduce the basic concepts, terms, and questions of Biology, Geology, Astronomy, Physics, & Chemistry over a three-year cycle.

Method. The basic procedure for each unit follows a sequence beginning with observation followed by a discussion to clarify the description of what is seen, concluded by a discussion of the reasons for the thing being the way it is—the attempt to explain. Drawings and descriptions are recorded along the way.

Philosophy. Careful observation is a basic skill of learning in all fields; it is not the unique purview of the "hard sciences." Indeed, learning to look carefully at the world has its place in the journey to wisdom; it is a first step upon one of the many ways that lead to God. It is morally educative in that it teaches us to humbly and honestly report what it is that we find, rather than what we wish to see. It is a source of great pleasure in that it is a nurturing and fulfillment of the basic desire that Aristotle observed in man, the desire to know, even as it responds to his natural wonder at the beauty of the world. In that wonder, we encounter the numinous—the unseen, mysterious spiritual implication that stands behind all that we can see. Further, as the students will learn later, sense experience precedes and provides the matter about which we reason in our logic classes. It is with these many ideas in mind that we select the basic goals for the science program here. Rather than favoring textbook provided overviews of the various facts and terms; we seek to bring the child into engagement with the real, foster his natural skills for seeing what is true, and allow him the opportunity to appreciate what is deeply good.

Presentations: To aid in introducing basic speech and presentation skills, students in these levels are expected to present at least once per year on a suitable science topic. For the most shy, this could be as simple as show-n-tell, but for others consider having poster and lap-book presentations to make it more formal.

Nature Journals: To aid in introducing the scientific method, students will record their observations in this workbook as a "Nature Journaling" which will be updated in each unit throughout the entire cycle. Nature journaling will have several assignment types from sketches and descriptions to observation records over the course of several days.

Teaching Tips: Lessons and Activities are provided in each unit. Lessons are designed as a discussion interaction between the teacher/parent and the child. This is a means of awakening thoughts about observations. The activities are meant to be practical assignments that further the discussion, either by way of learning vocabulary or by way of recording observations (Nature Journaling).

- Pay close attention to needed materials by looking ahead throughout the year! Sometimes you will need to order or collect materials before doing the lesson, and you want to have the time.
- We recommend that lessons be held outdoors as much as possible. The focus of Cycle 2 Science K-1 is Earth Science, so being outdoors will contribute to the experience as they learn facts.
- The Schola Rosa science program teaches scientific skills of observation and experiment through the Socratic Method --- guiding students by discussion to come to certain realizations about the natural world. Though your discussion may vary from what is provided here, be sure to follow the order of items as closely as possible.
- Try not to give students the definitions of terms at the beginning of a lesson, but do guide them toward a definition that they will understand and define themselves by the end of the lesson.

Recommended Read-Aloud Books to Accompany this Workbook (provided in online suite):

1. *Story Book of Science* by Jean Henri Fabre
2. *Madame How and Lady Why* by Charles Kingsley
3. *Home Geography* by C.C. Long

Unit 1: Layers of the Earth

- ☐ LESSON A: Observation and Discussion
  - o Read the lesson carefully to make sure you have all needed supplies and you understand the content.
  - o Observation Record: Ask your student to Draw his/her observation below and label the parts of the peach using the terms below.
- ☐ ACTIVITY A: Focus on Vocabulary
  - o Ask the student to find an object inside the house or outside in the yard that can be used as a model to show Earth's layers just like the peach from Lesson A. Draw and label the object found and compare it to the illustration of the Earth. Color the pictures.
- ☐ ACTIVITY B: Nature Journaling
  - o Have your student draw a picture of his or her house on top of the earth's crust and then the layers beneath.
  - o Help the student with proportion of layers.
- ☐ PARENT NOTES:

____

____

____

____

____

____

____

Lesson A: Model of the Earth's Layers

Objectives:

1. To identify the different layers of the Earth using a model.
2. To compare and contrast Earth's layer and the model.
3. To make predictions about the inside of the Earth.

Before the Lesson:

- ☐ Conduct science outside, whenever possible—check the lesson type and the weather.
- ☐ Gather and prep materials.

Materials Needed:

- ☐ 1/2 of a peach per student
- ☐ Picture of the cross-section of the Earth showing the Different layers
- ☐ Observation sheet (after the Lesson)
- ☐ Writing materials (pencil and colored pencils)

In Class:

Class Observation:

1. Have the students sit in a semi-circle in front of you outside.
2. Pull out a globe and use it to ask the students about the shape of the Earth. Explain that a globe is a model of the Earth. Ask the students what object they know that is the same shape as the Earth. *Answers could be a ball, fruits such as cherry or apple, egg etc.*
3. Then, ask the students if they know what is underneath the ground. Did you ever imagine what the earth is like beneath our feet? Write on the board the student's predictions.
4. Explain that the Earth is divided into layers.
5. Pull out a knife and cut the peach in half and explain that we are using the peach as a model to observe the layers of the Earth.

6. Showing the inside of the peach, ask the students to predict the number of layers that the Earth has.

- Point out to students the first layer, the CRUST. Ask students what they notice about the thickness of the crust.

  The crust is the outermost layer of the Earth. There are two types of crust: the CONTINENTAL CRUST is the solid ground we stand on, some of the hills and mountains we see around us; and the OCEANIC CRUST is the sea floor underneath our oceans. Ask to compare and contrast the skin of the peach and the actual Earth's crust (using a picture). Are there any differences? Are there any similarities? *The peach skin is very thin which is similar to the Earth's crust compared to the other layers. The skin of the peach which is just one layer doesn't show the two types of crust mentioned above.*

- Now, show students the second layer, the MANTLE, the fiery inside of the earth. What can students say about the thickness of the mantle?

  The mantle is the thickest part of the Earth's layer and is made up of molten rocks. Ask to compare and contrast the flesh of the peach and the actual Earth's mantle (using a picture). Are there any differences? Are there any similarities? *The flesh of the peach is the thickest part of the fruit which is similar to the Earth's mantle. The flesh of the peach is solid while the actual mantle is molten like a heavy thick syrup (ex. Honey or corn syrup).*

- Finally, show students the seed itself, the INNER CORE, and the dark red part directly near the seed, the OUTER CORE. What can students observe about the seed?

  The CORE is the innermost section of the Earth. It is also the densest layer.

7. Encourage students to share their observations about the peach.

Class Processing:

- Instruct students to return to a desk or to remain on the ground with binders (if outside).
- Hand-out the observation record and colored pencils.
- Give each student ½ of peach and review the different layers of the Earth as the students point them out using the peach.

- Instruct the students to draw what they see on their observation paper. Encourage them to look closely at each layer and to imagine the earth below them.
- Label the picture that the student draw using the terms learned (Crust, Mantle, Outer core and Inner core).
- They may eat the peach when they are finished!

Lesson Extension:

- Talk about the actual thickness of each Earth's layers using some reference point.
- How do you imagine the length of a mile? (Have a reference ready: e.g. from the Church to the corner of Elm is one mile long.)
- Now imagine that length times 20 to 30!!!! That is like driving from (city name) to (city name)!
- Talk about how temperature and pressure changes as you go deeper into the Earth's core.

Observation Record: Model of the Earth's Layer Using Peach

CRUST **MANTLE** **INNER CORE** **OUTER CORE**

Activity A: Compare and Contrast

Cross Section of the Earth

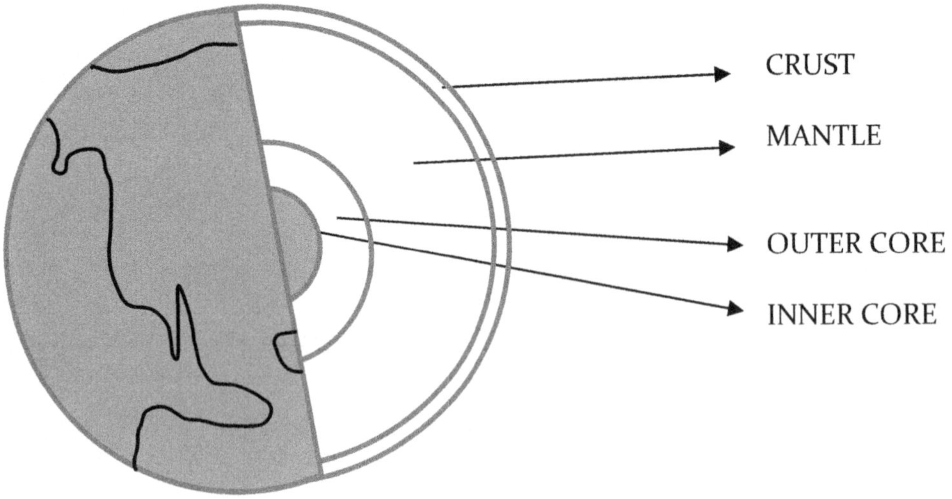

My Model

Activity B: My House on Top of Earth's Layers

Date: ______________________________

Unit 2: How Mountains Grow

- ☐ LESSON A: Observation and Discussion
  - Read the lesson carefully to make sure you have all needed supplies and you understand the content.
  - Five Types of Mountains: Identify the different types of mountains based on how each one of them are formed. Trace the name of each type of mountain.
- ☐ ACTIVITY A: Focus on Vocabulary
  - Memory Game! Cut out the pictures from "Five Types of Mountains" as well as from Activity A and glue them to cardstock. Use the pictures to play a memory game to review the different types of mountain formations.
- ☐ ACTIVITY B: Nature Journaling
  - Have your student draw a picture of any hills or mountains in your area.
- ☐ PARENT NOTES:

Lesson A: How Mountains Grow

Objectives:

1. To observe land forms particularly mountains or hills found in a particular area.
2. To identify the different processes that are involve in mountain formation.
3. To compare and contrast the various processes involved in mountain formation.

Before the Lesson:

1. Conduct science outside, whenever possible—check the lesson type and the weather.
2. Gather and prep materials.

Materials Needed:

- ☐ globe
- ☐ hard-boiled egg
- ☐ 4 piece of graham crackers per student
- ☐ 2 dollops of marshmallow fluff per student
- ☐ Paper plate
- ☐ clay
- ☐ "Five Types of Mountain Formation"
- ☐ Writing materials (pencil and colored pencils)

In Class:

Class Observation

- Have the students sit in a semi-circle in front of you outside.
- Tell the students to imagine riding an airplane or hot air balloon, then ask what are some of the things we can see looking down towards the Earth's surface. This is also a good time to review last week's lesson about the layers of the Earth. Remind the student that the layer that we see from above is the Earth's crust.

  Is the surface of the Earth flat? Or are there some bumps and valleys? You can also show aerial pictures from books to guide the students in the observation process.

- Tell the students that for this week, we are going to focus on one of the Earth's land feature which are the mountains. Ask the students if they know how mountains are formed. Show them a cracked hard-boiled egg and explain that the Earth's crust is just like the shell of the egg, (a) it is thin compared to the other layers, (b) it is the outermost layer, and (c) that the crust of the Earth just like the hard-boiled egg has cracks as well. Introduce the term "plates". Plates are the big pieces of the Earth's crust that move relative to one another.
- Given this information, explain that we would use a model to explain how mountains are formed. Explain that the graham crackers are just like the plates. Plates float above the thick molten magma of the mantle which is the marshmallow fluff.

    i. Lay the graham crackers side by side on top of the fluff and slide them in opposite direction. Observe what happened. One cracker can slide over the other forming a 'fault-block mountain'.

    ii. Next, before laying the graham crackers on top of the fluff, dip one end of both crackers in water, then ask the students to push the graham crackers (plates) towards each other. Again observe what happened. This time, the crackers will make 'fold mountain'.

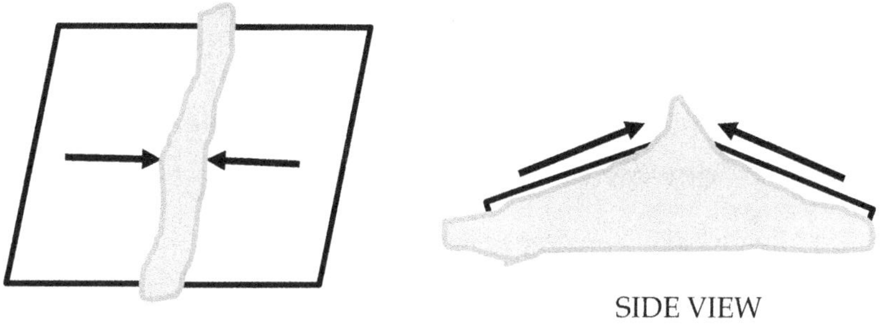

Class Processing:

- Using "Five Types of Mountain Formation" ask the students to identify which of the five types of formation is shown by the Graham Cracker Model?

    1. *Fault-block mountain, (b) Fold mountain*

- This time give students a pencil and piece of clay and ask them to make it thin and flat. Tell them that the clay is the crust and the pencil is the molten magma underneath. Explain that since magma is hotter and less dense it always wants to find a way to go to the surface. Push the pencil from underneath the thin clay making sure not making any hole, until it forms a dome shape structure.

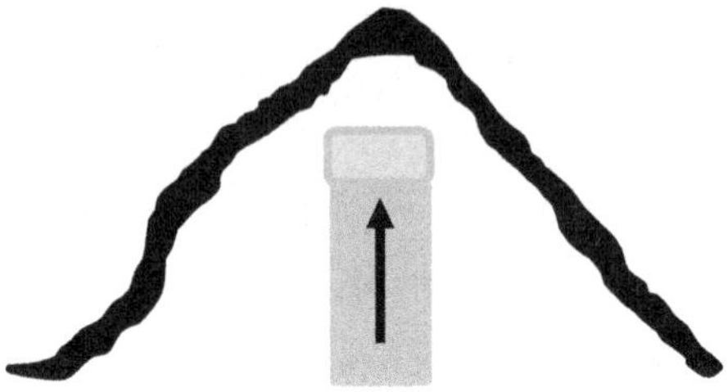

What happens when you push the clay from underneath?

It will make a dome mountain. Identify which is a dome mountain.

This time have the students push the pencil (magma) all the way through.

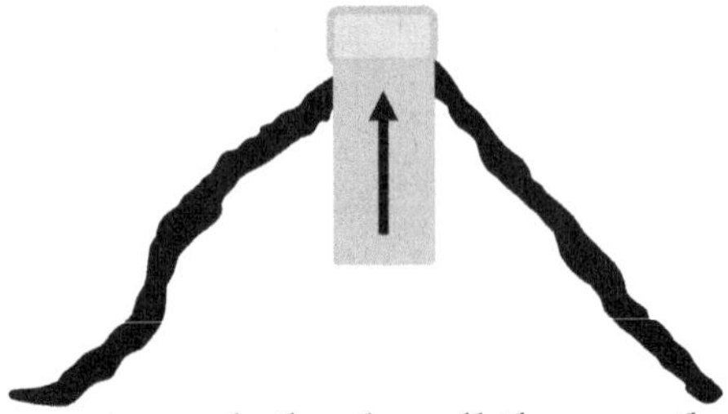

What happens when you push the clay all the way through from underneath using the eraser end of the pencil making a hole to the dome shape?

It will make a volcano. Identify which is a volcanic mountain.

- Next, have the students make a mountain shape with their clay and using the eraser end of a pencil, ask the students to push the peak of the mountain downwards.

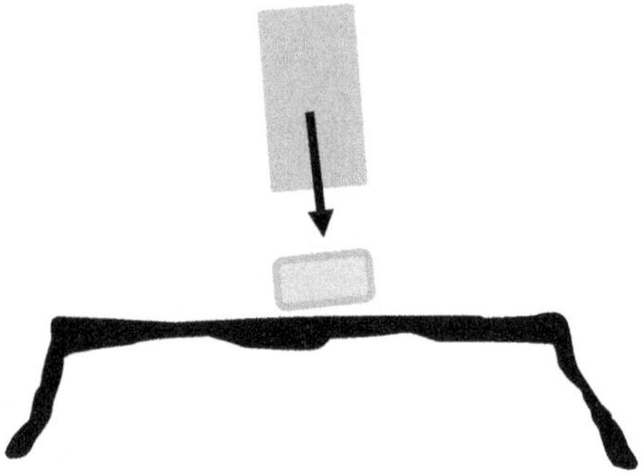

What happens when you push the clay downwards?

It will make a plateau. Identify which is a plateau.

Lesson Extension:

- Discuss what could be some forces (downwards) that can cause mountains to become a plateau. You can explore different agents of weathering and erosion such as wind and rain

Five Types of Mountains

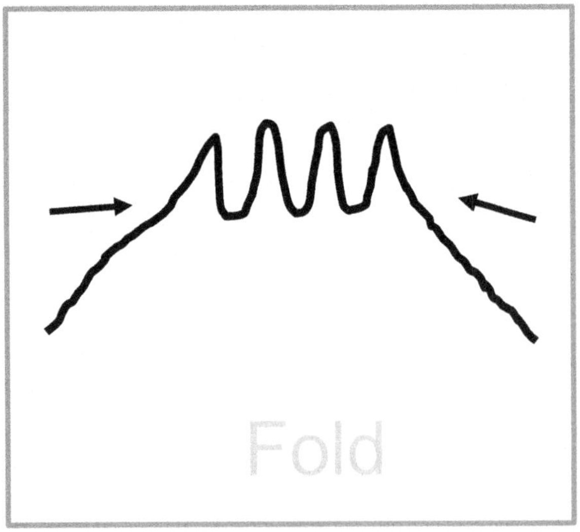

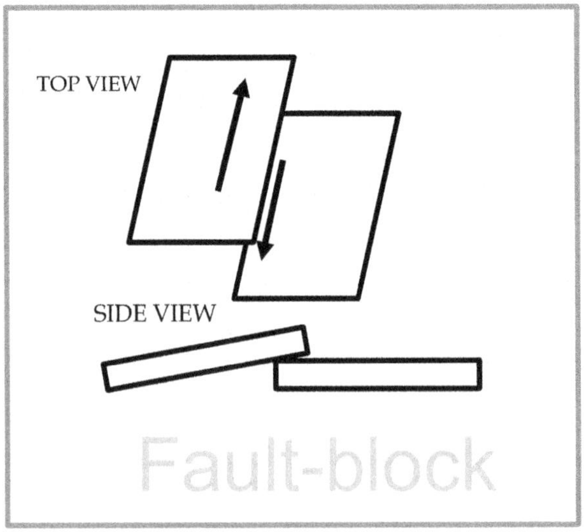

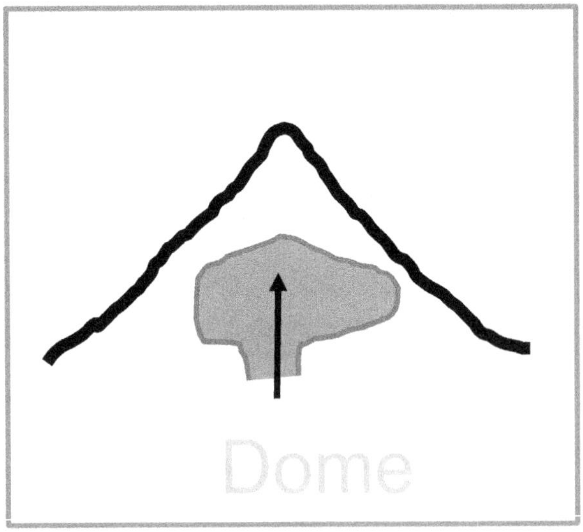

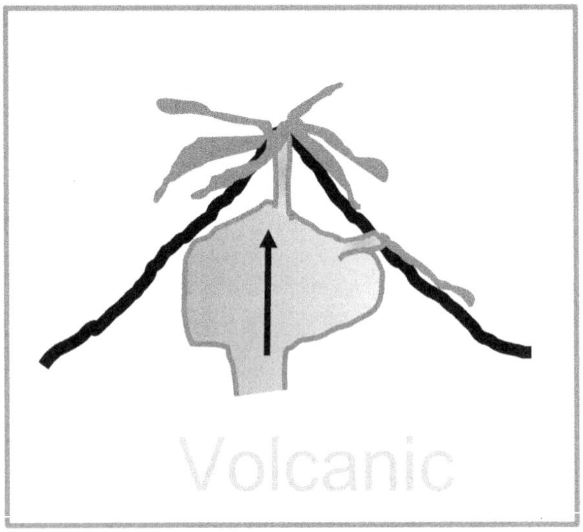

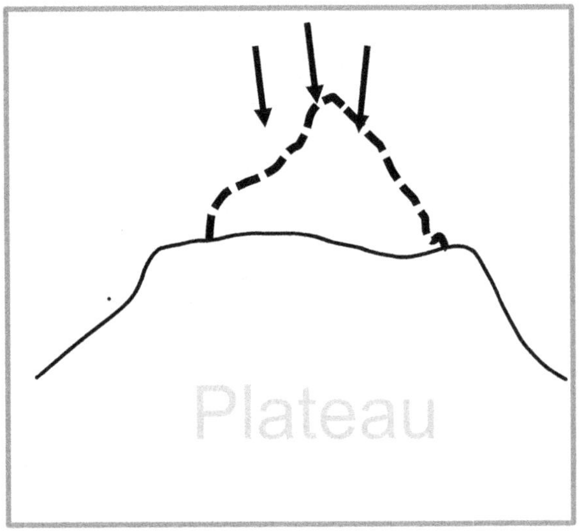

Activity A: Memory Game

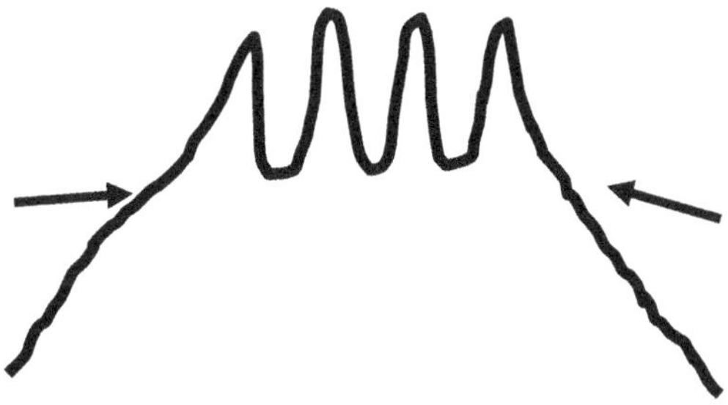

Fold

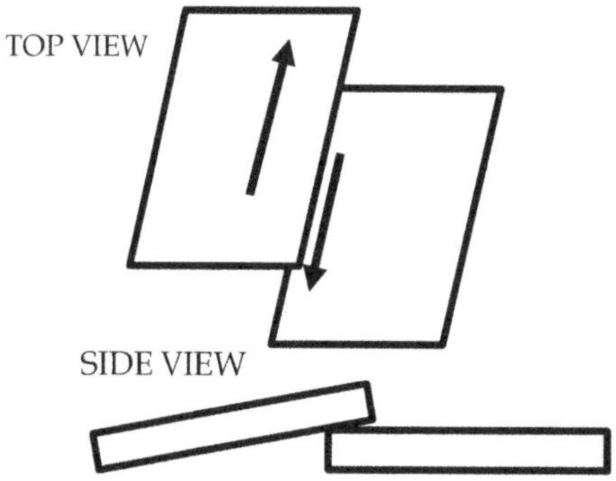

Fault-blocked

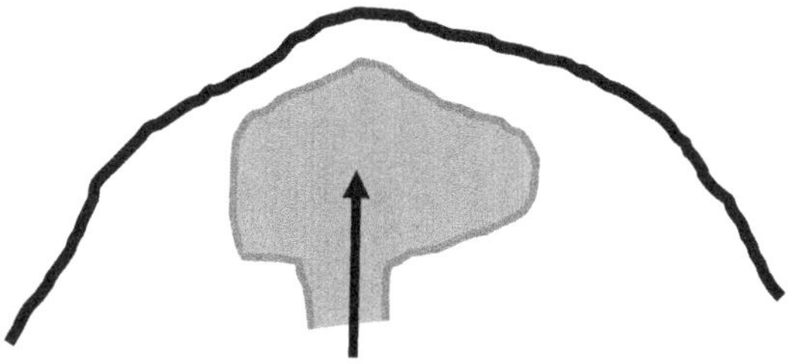

Dome

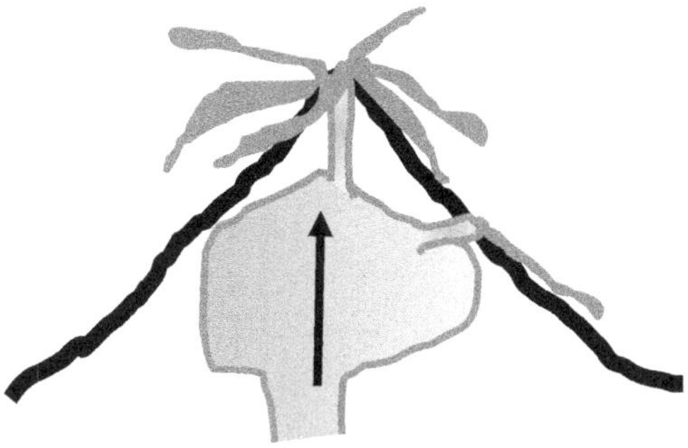

Volcanic

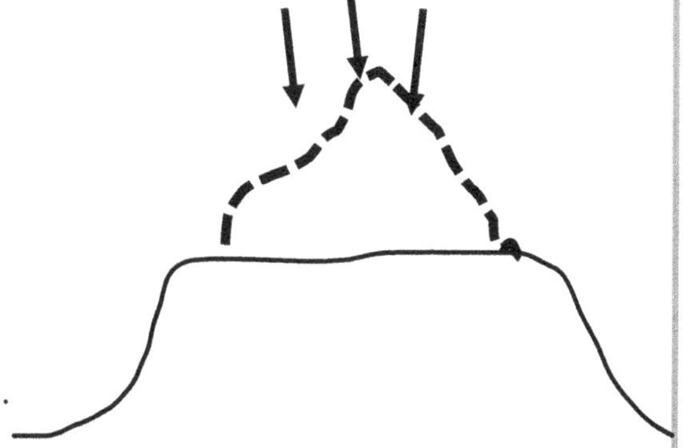

Plateau

Activity B: My Picture of a Mountain or Hill

Date: ______________________________

Unit 3: A Model Volcano

- ☐ LESSON A: Observation and Discussion
    - o Read the lesson carefully to make sure you have all needed supplies and you understand the content.
- ☐ ACTIVITY A: Focus on Vocabulary
    - o The different types of volcanoes result from the different materials that each type extruded and the type of eruption that can take place.
    - o Match the picture of the different types of volcanoes with the description.
- ☐ ACTIVITY B: Nature Journaling
    - o Students cannot exactly go out and draw the inside of a volcano, so an illustration has been provided.
    - o Color the illustration of a volcano.
    - o Cut and paste. Match the label for the different parts of a volcano shown by the arrow.
- ☐ PARENT NOTES:

____

____

____

____

____

____

____

Lesson A: A Model Volcano

Objectives:

1. To identify the different parts of a volcano.
2. To determine and differentiate types of volcanoes.
3. To determine how volcano erupts.

Before the Lesson:

- ☐ Conduct science outside, whenever possible—check the lesson type and the weather.
- ☐ Gather and prep materials.

Materials Needed:

- ☐ Film canister
- ☐ soda
- ☐ seltzer tablets
- ☐ cardboard
- ☐ playdough or clay
- ☐ tape
- ☐ small plastic or glass container (a narrower mouth would be ideal)
- ☐ ½ c water
- ☐ ¼ c vinegar
- ☐ ¼ c liquid detergent
- ☐ 2tbsp baking soda wrapped in tissue paper

In Class:

Class Observation

1. Have the students sit in a semi-circle in front of you outside.
2. Show your students a picture of a volcano and a mountain. Ask the students what is the difference between the two. The outside appearance might be very similar since volcano is a type of a mountain (a good way to review last week's lesson about mountains) but if we look at the interior of a volcano,

what would we see? Have the students recall how volcanic mountains are formed.

3. Tell the students that for this week, we are going to focus on one of the Earth's land feature which are the volcanoes and that we will be making a model of a volcano and create an eruption.

   Gather your materials for making a volcano. You can have the students work in pairs or groups of three.

   First make the cone shape mountain using cardboard. The cone shape cardboard should have a hole at the tapering end that should be the same size as the opening of the plastic bottle. Make sure that the cardboard covers the whole bottle. Tape the edges and place brown, green or grey playdough to cover the outer layer of the cone mountain to resemble the appearance of a volcanic mountain.

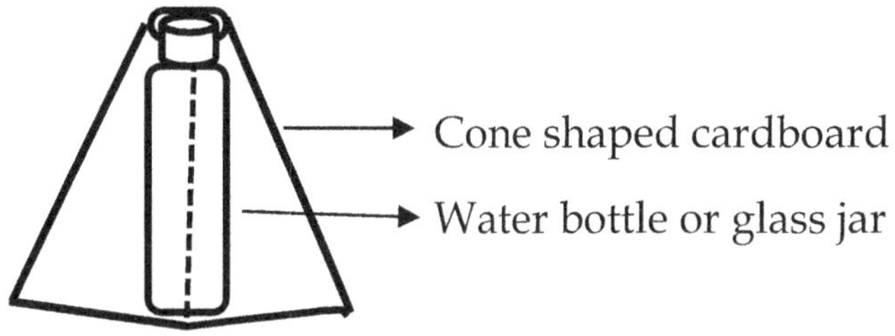

   Explain to the students that the water bottle represents the magma chamber where molten rocks or 'magma' are concentrated. The narrow end of the water bottle represents the main vent or 'throat' of the volcano where lava (magma that reaches the surface) and other volcanic debris such as gas, ash and rocks are expelled or extruded.

   Next, is to create the magma mixture. Combine the water, vinegar and dish soap and place them inside the bottle. Ask the students what makes the rocks melt to create magma? *Due to high pressure and temperature underneath the Earth's layers.*

   Explain to the students that a lot of gas is trapped underneath the Earth's crust when rocks melt to form magma. As a result the gas underneath volcanoes would want to escape so if you have too much gas underneath, it can create too much pressure causing the eruption to happen.

   To demonstrate, fill the film canister half way with soda, then place quarter of seltzer tablet. Place the cover and put on the ground upside down. Observe what happens. After few seconds, the film canister will pop and fly upwards similar to a volcanic eruption. This demonstration should be done outdoors or a room with high ceiling.

Lastly, to erupt their model volcano, wrap baking soda in a tissue and drop it inside the bottle with the magma mixture. Observe what happens.

Class Processing:

1. Ask the students if they observe any difference between the film canister eruption and their model volcano eruption.

   Which model erupts violently and which model show a less violent eruption?

   What can cause the difference in the intensity of eruption on actual volcanoes?

Lesson Extension:

- Look at a topographic map and locate different volcanoes around the world. Look for patterns where the volcanoes are located. Compare and contrast volcanoes made through subduction zones and hot spots.

Activity A: Types of Volcanoes

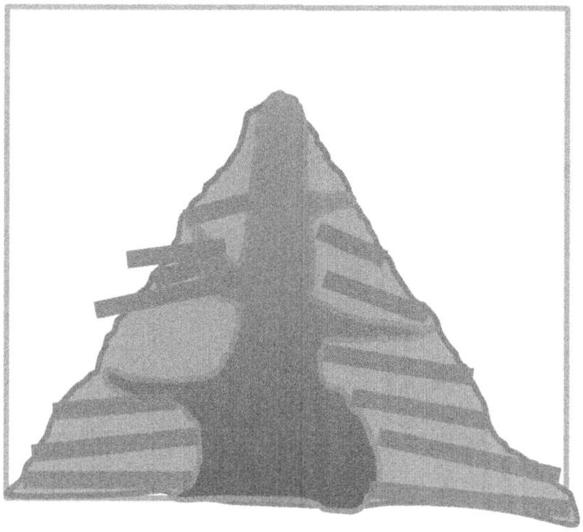

CINDER CONES

This type of volcano is small, steeped side cones that can caused explosive eruption due to gas formation.

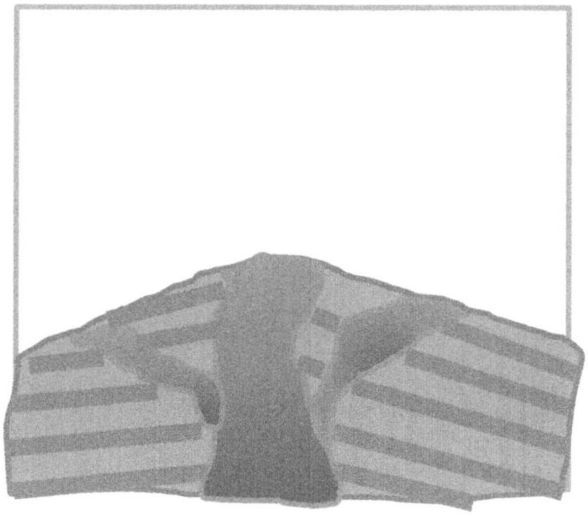

COMPOSITE or STRATOVOLCANO

This type of volcano is large, symmetrical cone shape and steeped sided. The volcano is made up of layers of lava, ash and cinder blocks. They can have violent eruption.

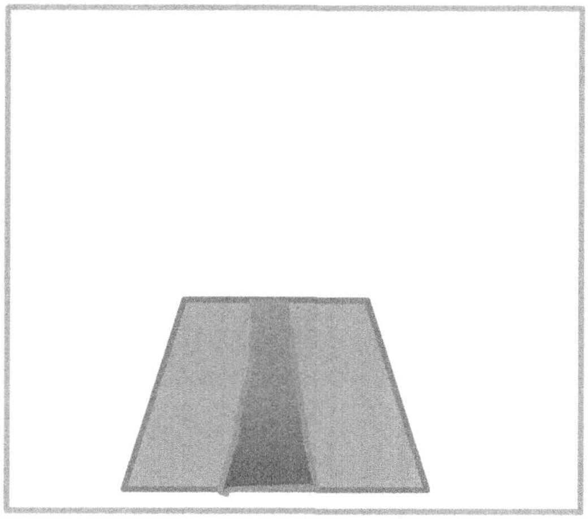

SHIELD

This type of volcano is large but low and has gently sloping sides. It does not erupt violently and form layers from hardened lava.

Activity B: Parts of a Volcano

Inside of a Volcano

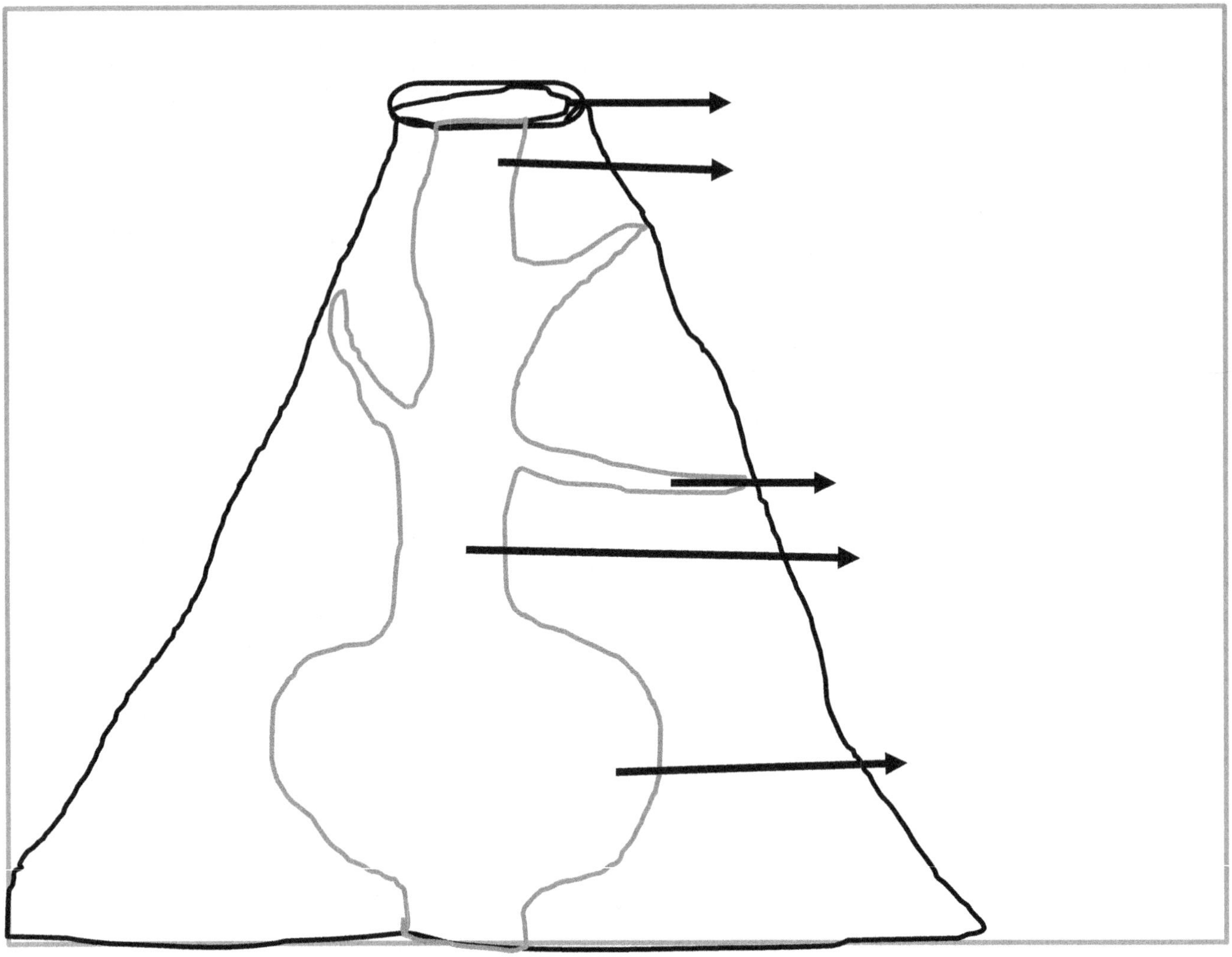

Magma chamber	Main Vent	Side Vent
Throat	Crater	

Unit 4: Earthquakes

- ☐ LESSON A: Observation and Discussion
  - Read the lesson carefully to make sure you have all needed supplies and you understand the content.
  - Observation Record: Comparing how different substrate affect the ground movement during earthquake. Draw observations before and after the shaking for the two types of substrate. Write observations in the space provided.
- ☐ ACTIVITY A: Focus on Vocabulary
  - The magnitude of an earthquake is determined by the seismograph and each scale of magnitude results to varying degree of damage to properties. Familiarize yourself with the chart and draw possible damage expected at various scales
- ☐ ACTIVITY B: Nature Journaling
  - Color the Earthquake Shaking Hazard Map in the United States (provided by USGS.gov). Then, complete the preparation tasks below the map.
- ☐ PARENT NOTES:

____

____

____

____

____

____

____

Lesson A: Earthquakes

Objectives:

1. To model how earthquake is generated.
2. To compare earthquake intensity with the type of resulting destruction.
3. To compare how different substrates affect ground movement.

Before the Lesson:

1. Conduct science outside, whenever possible—check the lesson type and the weather.
2. Gather and prep materials.

Materials Needed:

- ☐ 2 books per student
- ☐ 2 plastic cups
- ☐ Soil and water
- ☐ Dry sand
- ☐ several coins to make about 2″ high when stacked on top of one another

In Class:

Class Observation:

PART A

1) Position 2 books on a table in front of students. Ask students what it is they see.

How would they describe it? Explain to students that the line in between the two books is a fault line! Ask them if they remember what can form at a fault line? *This is a good time to review plate tectonics and various plate boundaries such as subduction zones, transform faults and oceanic ridges.*

2) Ask students what they think will happen if the books representing two tectonic

plates move at the fault line. Tell students you are going to try it! Move the books at opposite direction, then repeat this step again after building a block town over the fault line. Begin with small movements and then increase movement. What happened? Ask students to describe what they observed.

PART B

1) Fill one plastic cup with soil about ¾ full. Add some water just enough to compress the soil. In the other cup place the dry sand. Stack the coin on top of the compacted soil and placed it on top of a vibrating phone for about 30secs. Observe how many of the coins fell off. Repeat the same process with the cup containing dry sand. Compare the number of coins that fell between the compacted soil and dry sand. Fill in your "Earthquake Observation Sheet ."

Class Processing:

What did you see?

Did the coins fall right away? Why not?

In which cup did you observe more effect of the vibration? The dry loose sand or the compacted soil?

Class Discussion:

Have you ever been in an earthquake?

Where did you feel it? (in person, on video, etc.?)

What was it like?

Were you scared?

Observation Record

COMPACTED SOIL

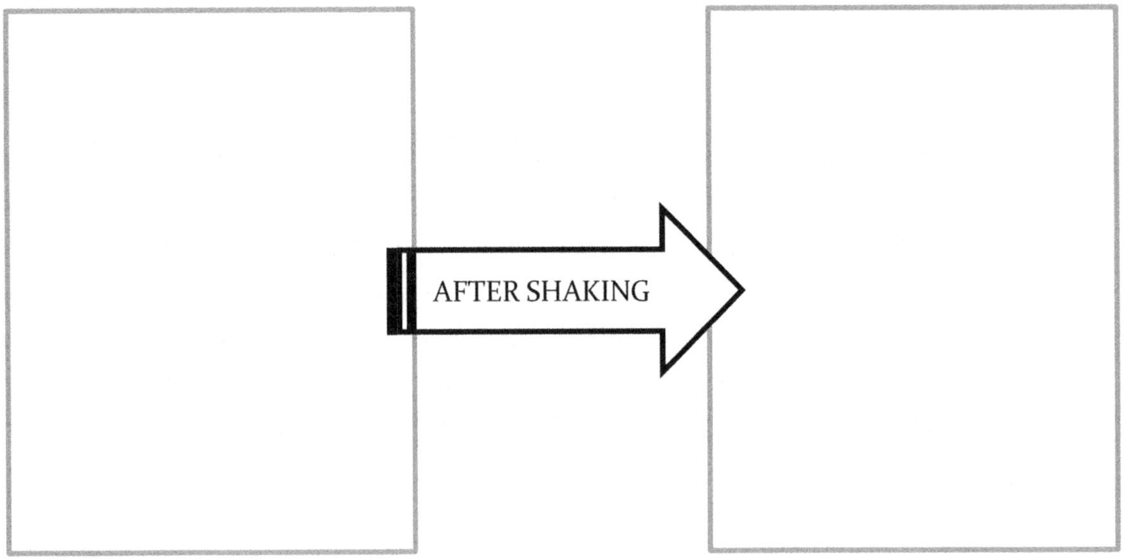

DRY LOOSE SAND

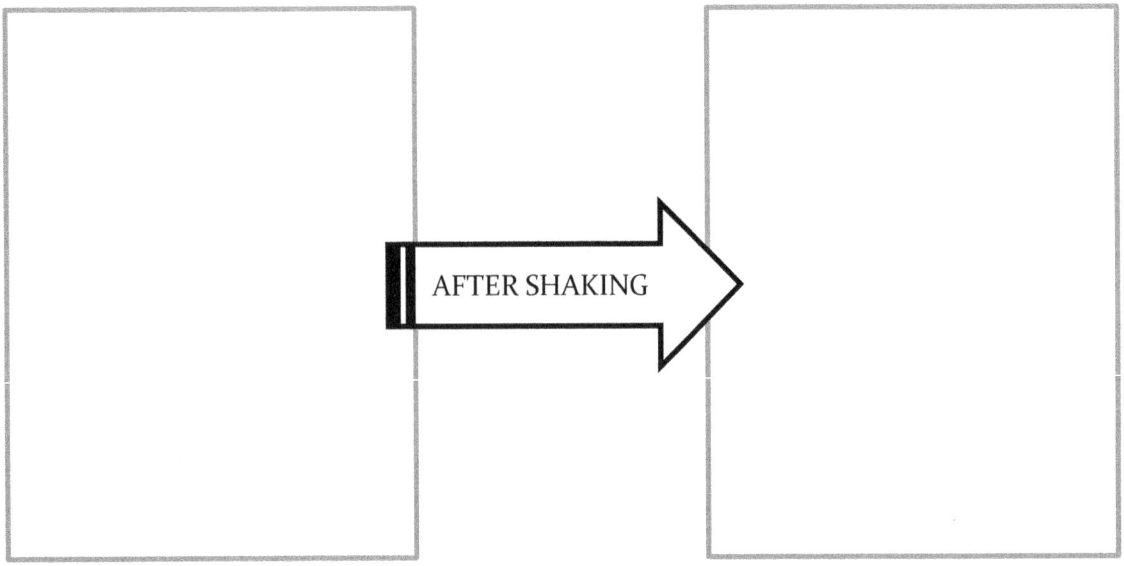

Circle the word that best describe your observation:

After shaking, there are *(less/more)* coins that fell down on the compacted soil.

After shaking there are *(less/more)* coins that fell down on the loose dry sand.

Activity A: Earthquake Magnitude Scale

Magnitude	Earthquake Effects	Draw your picture
0-2.9	Not felt, recorded by a seismograph	
3.0-3.9	Felt but no damage (Swinging of ceiling lights)	
4.0-4.9	Felt by all and can cause very minor damage (Cracked wall)	
5.0-5.9	Damage to weak structures (Movement of furniture)	
6.0-7.9	Major damage over large areas (Buildings collapsed)	
8.0 and higher	Can totally destroy communities close to the center of the earthquake (Total destruction of buildings, bridges and roads)	

Activity B: Earthquake Hazard Map

Earthquake Shaking Hazards in the United States

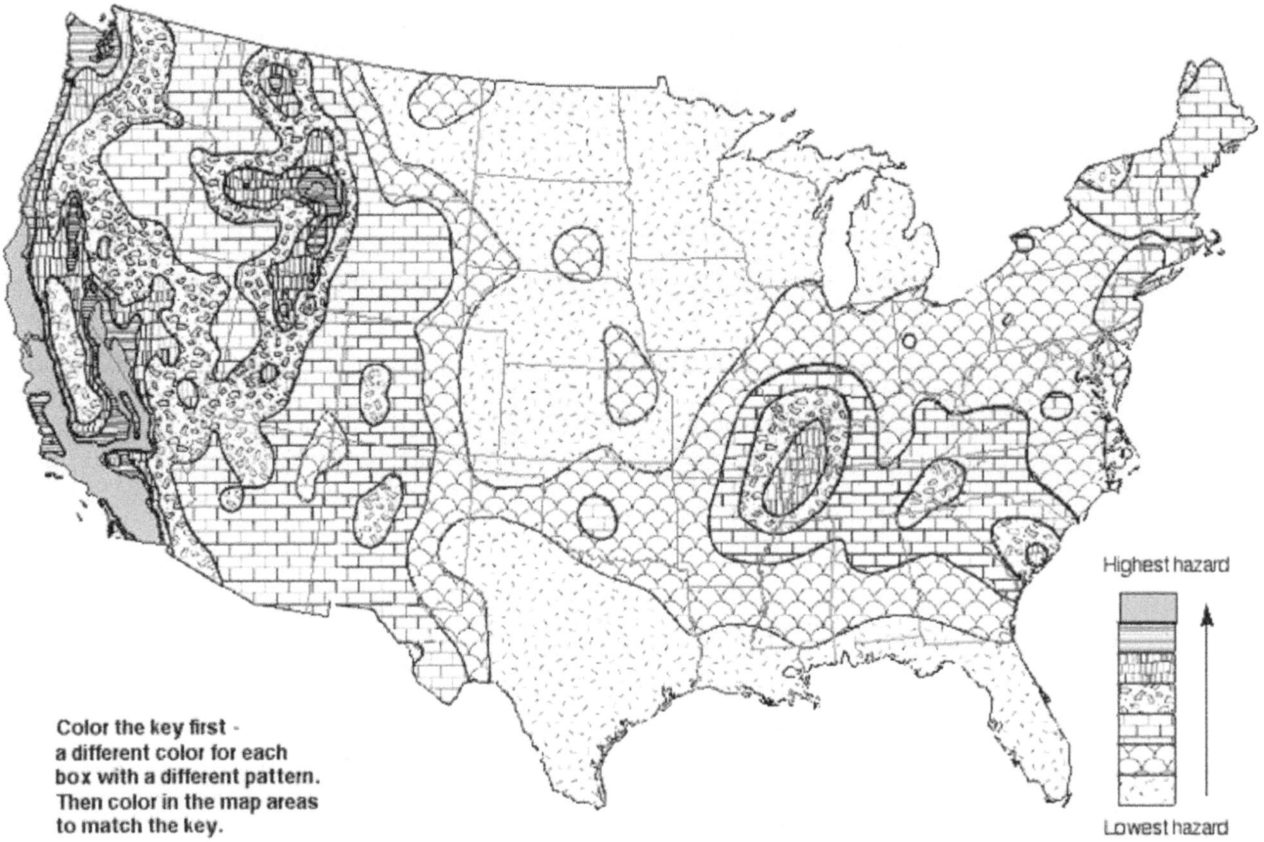
Color the key first -
a different color for each
box with a different pattern.
Then color in the map areas
to match the key.
Highest hazard
Lowest hazard

Locate your state in the map and identify the hazard that you might encounter during an earthquake.

Discuss with your family what steps you can do in an event of an earthquake.

Do an earthquake drill: Practice the *Drop, Cover, and Hold* (FEMA)

a. Get under the table or desk.

b. Turn away from the windows.

c. Put both hands on the back of your neck.

d. If your desk or table moves, hold onto the legs and move with it.

Unit 5: Types of Rocks

- ☐ LESSON A: Observation and Discussion
  - Read the lesson carefully to make sure you have all needed supplies and you understand the content.
  - Observation Record: Draw inside the box what you observe from the activity.
- ☐ ACTIVITY A: Nature Journaling
  - Complete the information for each rock that you collect.
  - Copy several copies of the pages and make a booklet for your rock collection. Cut along broken lines and fold along solid line.
  - Use an egg carton to keep your rock collection and label the rocks using permanent marker.
- ☐ ACTIVITY B: Focus on Vocabulary
  - Word Search. Find the words provided in the word search.
- ☐ PARENT NOTES:

Lesson A: Types of Rocks

Objectives:

1. To observe and classify different types of rocks.
2. To compare and contrast the different types of rocks.
3. To learn how the different types of rocks are formed.

Before the Lesson:

1. Conduct science outside, whenever possible—check the lesson type and the weather.
2. Gather and prep materials.

Materials Needed:

- ☐ collection of different rocks (ask the students to bring 3-6 rocks each to bring to class)
- ☐ samples of Igneous, Sedimentary and Metamorphic Rocks. If actual samples are not available, print colored pictures for each type of rocks.
- ☐ A handful of 3-4 color shavings (you can use pencil sharpener and collect the color shavings and keep them in separate baggies)
- ☐ Tin foil
- ☐ Hot water
- ☐ Plastic bin (shoe box size)
- ☐ Muffin cups
- ☐ Oven or microwave

In Class:

Class Observation:

PART A

1) Observe the rocks that the children brought to class. Focus on color, texture, shape, weight and any interesting feature of the rocks.
2) Pick one to do in class together and the students can do the rest of the recordings at home. This is a good way to introduce how to keep rocks using egg carton and labeling them properly.

Use the Observation Record "Rock Collection" to fill in the information.

3) Discuss how rocks may look and feel differently and this is because different rocks are made up of different 'ingredients' and from different processes.

PART B (the teacher can do a demonstration of this activity and have the students help with the activity).

4) Introduce the three types of rocks (Igneous, Sedimentary and Metamorphic Rocks). Tell the kids that we will learn these three types of rocks in details in coming weeks. For this week the class will focus on how these three types or rocks are formed.

5) Give each students a 6x6in square tin foil and placed the shaved crayons in the middle. Tell the students that the crayon shavings are just like the rock sediments or small pieces of rocks and dirt we see around us. Fold the tinfoil around the shavings and using a rolling pin press the shavings flat. Open the foil and have students describes what happened to the crayon shavings.

   This is a sedimentary rock. Sedimentary rocks are made when sediments are carried and deposited in a low lying basin like a river bed and then subjected to high pressure (compaction or squashed together) forming this type of rock.

   You can show the students an example of sedimentary rocks and discuss its characteristics, comparing it with the compacted crayon they created.

6) Then fold the aluminum foil again containing the 'sedimentary rock' and placed it in the plastic bin containing hot water. Wait for 2-3 minutes before taking it from the hot water. As the students wait, they can start filling out their observation sheet "Types of Rocks".

   Take the aluminum foil with 'sedimentary rocks' in it from the hot water and placed it on a dish or paper towel and run the rolling pin again before opening the foil.

   Ask the students if the 'sedimentary rock' undergone a change.

   This is now a metamorphic rock. Metamorphic rocks are made when rocks are subjected to high pressure (pressing of the rolling pin) and high temperature (submerging in hot water) resulting to the change in the physical appearance and chemical composition of the previous rock/s resulting to the metamorphic rock.

   The students should be able to observe that some of the crayons have melted creating a more blending of the colors.

You can show the students an example of metamorphic rock and discuss its characteristics, comparing it with the partially melted crayon they created.

7) Placed the 'metamorphic rocks that the students created in individual muffin cups and place them in an oven at 350oF until all the crayons have melted, for about 2-3 minutes.

   As the students wait, they can start filling out their observation sheet "Types of Rocks".

   After 3 minutes, show the students the resulting 'rock'

   Ask the students to described what happened to the 'metamorphic rock.

   This is now an igneous rock. Igneous rocks are made when any types of rocks are subjected to really high temperature (placing in an oven) resulting to the melting of rocks forming magma and solidifying as igneous rocks when cools down.

   You can show the students an example of igneous rock and discuss its characteristics, comparing it with the totally melted crayon as a result of putting 'metamorphic rock' in the oven.

Class Processing:

Ask students what are the different colors of the rocks they have brought. How about the texture? Have students choose their largest and smallest rock; lightest and heaviest. Explain centimeter if necessary.

Class Discussion:

Invite students to start their rocks collection this week. The rocks collection would be an on-going activity for Units 5-8. Each student is encouraged to collect 4-6 rocks for their collection and record information in their booklet (Activity A Observation Record). Keep collected rocks in egg cartons. Assig a number for each rock and make sure that it is corresponding to the number in their booklet.

Each week, invite students to show any interesting rock they find and share information that they recorded in their Rock Collection Booklet.

Observation Record: Rock Collection

Sedimentary Rock

Shaved crayons represent sediments. Sedimentary rocks are made when sediments are carried and deposited in a low-lying basin like a river bed and then subjected to high pressure (compaction or squashed together) forming this type of rock.

Examples: Sandstone, limestone, shale

Metamorphic Rock

Metamorphic rocks are made when rocks are subjected to high pressure (pressing of the rolling pin) and high temperature (submerging in hot water) resulting to the change in the physical appearance and chemical composition of the previous rock/s.

Examples: marble, gneiss, schist

Igneous Rock

Igneous rocks are made when any types of rocks are subjected to really high temperature (placing in an oven) resulting to the melting of rocks forming magma and solidifying as igneous rocks when cools down.

Examples: granite, basalt, obsidian, pumice

Activity A: Rock Collection Booklet

My Rock Collection Booklet

____

NAME

Rock Number: ______________	My additional notes:
Date: ___________________________ ___________________________	
Where I found the rock: ____________ ___________________________ ___________________________ ___________________________ ___________________________ ___________________________	
Color: ___________________________ ___________________________	
Texture: check anything that applies ○ Smooth ○ Rough ○ Many holes ○ Grainy	My picture of the rock:
Size: ___________ cm.	

Note: In measuring the circumference of a rock, wrap around the measuring tape on the widest part of the rock. You can also use a string to wrap around the rock and measure the length of the string using a regular ruler to find the circumference.

Activity B: Word Search

L	X	C	Q	F	O	G	Q	U	B	V	V	W	B	F
R	N	O	I	T	A	C	I	F	I	H	T	I	L	O
Z	X	G	S	H	E	B	A	S	A	L	T	S	Y	C
W	N	S	N	K	P	L	V	D	O	M	M	R	D	E
R	S	S	L	E	C	N	A	Y	H	X	E	Z	I	L
Q	O	E	T	A	I	O	K	H	W	L	T	S	Z	C
I	U	D	D	V	T	S	R	R	S	A	A	P	R	Y
L	R	I	Y	I	N	E	S	J	N	V	M	U	R	C
L	S	M	J	E	M	T	D	X	G	A	O	M	V	K
G	U	E	P	X	A	E	M	Q	C	L	R	I	H	C
A	O	N	L	G	A	Y	N	M	D	J	P	C	Z	O
M	E	T	R	X	T	S	L	T	B	I	H	E	A	R
G	N	A	A	W	X	L	G	M	S	O	I	J	K	S
A	G	R	D	C	Z	T	U	F	C	Y	C	K	A	A
M	I	Y	E	N	O	T	S	D	N	A	S	P	E	M

Basalt
Gneiss
Igneous
Lava
Lithification
Magma
Metamorphic

Rocks
Sandstone
Sedimentary
Sediments
Shale
Slate
Pumice

Rock Cycle

Unit 6: Igneous Rocks

- ☐ LESSON A: Observation and Discussion
    - o Read the lesson carefully to make sure you have all needed supplies and you understand the content.
    - o Observation Record: Draw inside the box what you observe from the activity. Complete each sentence by identifying the missing word.
- ☐ ACTIVITY A: Nature Journaling
    - o See Unit 5 Activity A for Rock Collecting Booklet. Complete the information for each IGNEOUS rock that you collect.
- ☐ ACTIVITY B: Focus on Vocabulary
    - o Color and study the diagram showing the formation of igneous rocks.
- ☐ PARENT NOTES:

____

____

____

____

____

____

Lesson A: Igneous Rocks

Objectives:

1) To identify different types of igneous rocks.
2) To compare and contrast different types of igneous rocks based in their physical appearance and formation.
3) To help students understand how the different processes of igneous rocks formation influence the rocks physical properties.

Before the Lesson:

- ☐ Conduct science outside, whenever possible—check the lesson type and the weather.
- ☐ Gather and prep materials.

Materials Needed:

- ☐ 1 Small paper cup per student.
- ☐ 1 Small paper cup (for adult to show example in)
- ☐ 3 Tbs. Corn syrup per student (per cup)
- ☐ 2-3 Bottles of food extract flavoring of your choice (vanilla extract, mint extract, etc.)
- ☐ 3-4 Small bottles of food coloring
- ☐ 1 Spoon per student (for mixing)
- ☐ 1 Tbs. for measuring the corn syrup
- ☐ 1 Microwaveable plate per classroom
- ☐ 1 Pot holder per classroom (for adult)
- ☐ 1 Household Microwave
- ☐ 1 Sheet of paper or Science Journal per student
- ☐ 1 Set of colored pencils per student
- ☐ 1 Pencil or writing utensil per student
- ☐ 1 -2 Books about igneous rocks (See Recommendations in Schola Rosa bookstore)
- ☐ ½ cup of sugar per student
- ☐ 1 Baking sheet per classroom
- ☐ 1 Candy thermometer per classroom (temp needs to reach 250 degrees to make a hard candy)

In Class:

1. Class Observation:
   - ☐ Ask students if they were able to find any igneous rocks when they were hunting for rocks last week.
   - ☐ Ask students to describe what an igneous rock looks like and to share anything they know about igneous rocks.
2. Class Processing:
   - ☐ Read or look at the pictures of the book about igneous rocks.
   - ☐ Show students a picture of the inside of a volcano and explain how geologists think igneous rocks were formed.
   - ☐ Tell students "igneous" means fire-ous. (Think of words like "ignite" and "ignition.")
   - ☐ Show students how to do hand motions to remember how igneous rocks are formed. (See Below)
   - ☐ Practice the hand motions a few times with the students.
3. Class Experiment ~ Igneous Candy Rocks
   - ☐ Invite students to gather around you as you demonstrate how igneous rocks are formed.
   - ☐ Set out one paper cup.
   - ☐ Tell students that the bowl is like the center of the Earth.
   - ☐ Measure out 3 tbs. of corn syrup into the paper cup.
   - ☐ Tell students the corn syrup represents the magma inside the Earth.
   - ☐ Add a drop of food flavoring extract of your choice and gently mix with the end of the handle end of the spoon.
   - ☐ Show students how thick the syrup is when cool.
   - ☐ Then, add a few drops of food coloring of your choice and barely swirl the color around in the corn syrup creating a wavy pattern.
   - ☐ Pour all the sugar onto the baking sheet so the metal is lightly covered.

☐ Place the corn syrup cup on the microwavable plate and place in microwave for 2 min. until the corn syrup is boiling hot and the temperature is at 250 degrees.

*N.B. It might boil over so be careful!

- Use a pot holder to remove the plate from the microwave.
- Allow students to observe the boiling corn syrup cup, NOT touch it!
- Tell students when the corn syrup became hot, it began to boil and push the corn syrup upwards. When the rock inside the Earth gets hot enough, it melts into magma.
- Quickly pour the boiling hot corn syrup onto the sugar.
- (Optional add one drop of food coloring to the cooling corn syrup and use the knife to make a design.)
- Explain to students that when the magna reaches the surface of the Earth, it changes to lava. As the hot lava cools, it forms rocks.
- Tell students that our magma (corn syrup) started out quite sticky and runny, but after it was heated and after the bubbles created pressure, it became a hard candy, an igneous candy rock.
- Once the igneous candy rock is cooled, rinse in cool water to get extra sugar off.
- Now, give each student a paper cup (with corn syrup pre-measured for large classes).
- Invite students to create their own igneous candy rock by experimenting with different flavors, colors, or other food items while the corn syrup is cool and sticky.
    - *N.B. for the younger student, an adult should add the flavoring and color. Remember a little goes a long way.
- Repeat the above steps with every student.
- Once the igneous candy rocks are cooled, encourage students to study their rock and try holding it up to the sunlight or lamp light.
- Ask students if they see any wavy lines, air bubbles, or shiny parts of the igneous candy rock.
- Hand out blank paper or a science journal, pencils, and colored pencils to students.
- Ask students to write or draw the different steps used to make the candy igneous rock. Give assistance to students who need help.
- Allow students to eat their own igneous candy rock

Observation Record: Igneous Rock Candy

Rock Candy Experiment

Molten rocks are called ☐☐☐☐☐ **.**

When magma cools and solidifies, it becomes ☐☐☐☐☐☐☐ **rocks.**

Activity B: Formation of Igneous Rocks

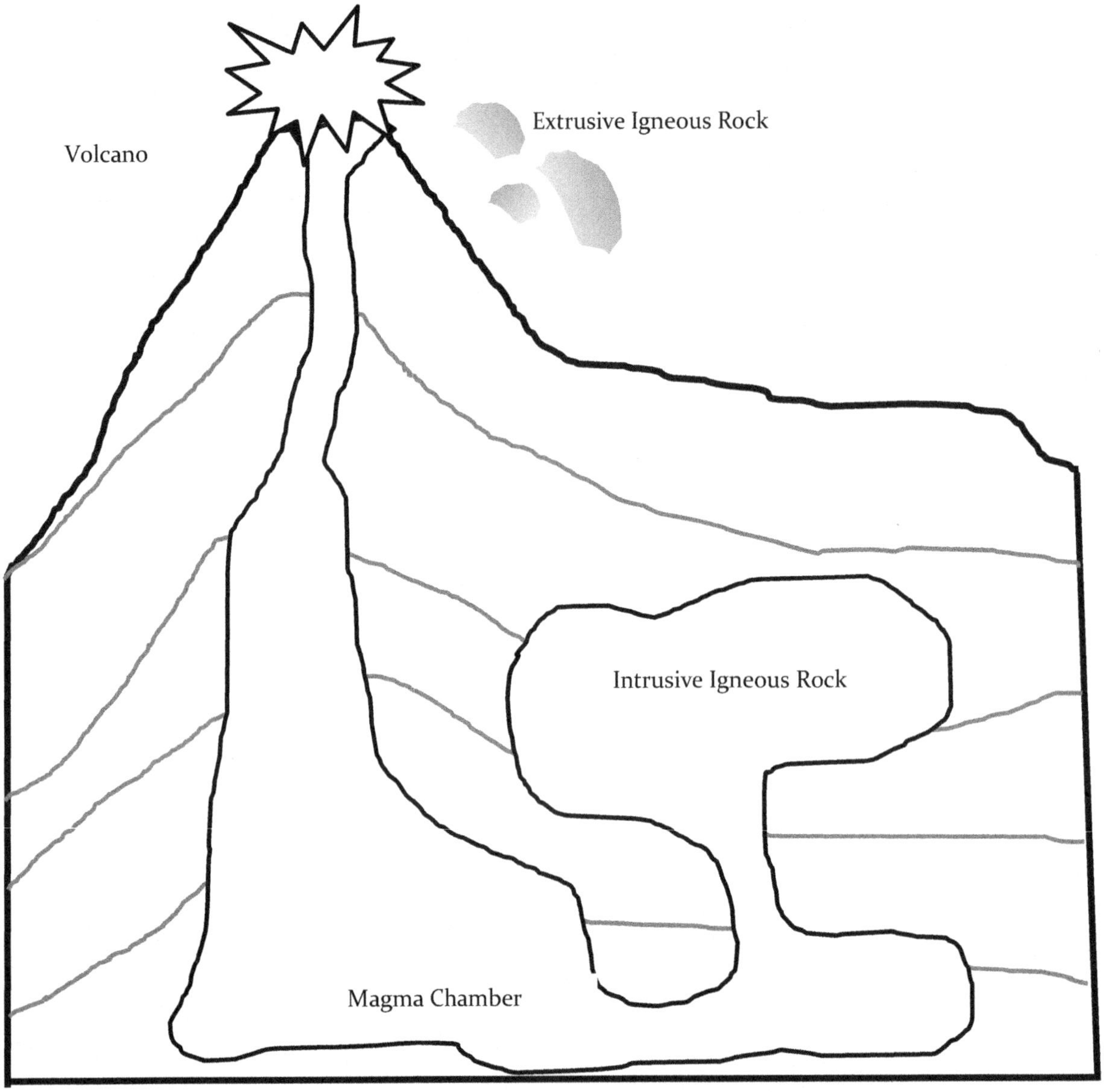

Unit 7: Sedimentary Rocks

- ☐ LESSON A: Observation and Discussion
  - o Read the lesson carefully to make sure you have all needed supplies and you understand the content.
  - o Observation Record: Draw what you observe from the activity. Color and label your picture.
- ☐ ACTIVITY A: Nature Journaling
  - o See Unit 5 Activity A for Rock Collecting Booklet. Complete the information for each SEDIMENTARY rock that you collect.
- ☐ ACTIVITY B: Focus on Vocabulary
  - o Color and study the diagram showing the formation of sedimentary rocks.
- ☐ PARENT NOTES:

Lesson A: Sedimentary Rocks

Objective:

This lesson introduces students to sedimentary rocks by helping them understand how they were made.

Before the Lesson:

- ☐ Conduct science outside, whenever possible—check the lesson type and the weather.
- ☐ Gather and prep materials.

Materials Needed:

☐ 1 packet of Jell-O per 6 students (increase amount based on class size)

☐ Water

☐ Water pitcher

☐ Ice

☐ 1 electric hot plate to boil water

☐ 1 pot for heating water

☐ 1 plate or pan that will fit over the bowl of Jell-O

☐ 1 large, glass bowl for Jell-O

☐ 1 quart-sized mason jar per 6 students (increase amount based on class size)

☐ 1 crushed graham cracker per 6 students (increase amount based on class size)

☐ ½ cup diced peaches (or other fruit) per 6 students (increase amount based on class size)

☐ ½ cup dried fruits or nuts per 6 students (increase amount based on class size)

☐ 1 book of your choice to illustrate sedimentary rocks

(See Recommendations in Schola Rosa bookstore)

☐ 1 sheet of paper or Science Journal per student

☐ 1 pencil per student

In Class:

1. Class Observation:

☐ Ask students what kinds of rocks they found at home.

☐ Were they able to find any sedimentary rocks last week?

☐ Allow students to describe their rocks and which ones they thought were sedimentary.

2. Class Processing:

☐ Show students a picture of the ocean and explain how scientists think sedimentary rocks were formed.

☐ What is "Sediment"? Where can you find sediment?

3. Class Experiment ~ Sediment in a Jar

☐ Invite students to gather around you as you demonstrate how sedimentary rocks are thought to be formed.

☐ Mix the Jell-O with the hot water until it dissolves, explaining that there is sand and dirt in all water, especially thinking of the sand in the ocean. At the bottom of the ocean, we can find volcanoes! Here there is heat and it can dissolve compound in the water.

☐ Now, mix in your cool water and talk about the sand cooling down and how changes in temperature can change the physical features of an object (remember the rock candy!).

☐ Begin to drop items into the Jell-O mixture along with the ice as you stir. Start with the diced fruit, then the dried fruit/nuts, and finally the graham cracker. Tell the students that these are pieces of sediments that were carried to the ocean when it rains.

Ask the students what can cause for rocks to break down into smaller pieces? *Weathering is a process that breaks down rocks, soil and minerals due to physical and chemical means.*

Ask the students what other ways these sediments end up in a body of water like the ocean? *Erosion is the transport of rocks, soil and minerals form one location to another due to natural agents (e.i. wind and water).*

Stir very well and set to the side to allow the Jell-O to set.

☐ Place a large plate or pan on top of the bowl to symbolize the "pressure of the above water," asking students to imagine how heavy the water above the bottom of the ocean must be on the ocean floor. *This process is called lithification which includes- a) COMPACTION- it happens when the overlying layers exert pressure on underlying layers causing the sediments to be tightly squeezed together, and b) CEMENTATION- it happens when dissolved minerals bind sediments together.*

□ While waiting, listen to the Science presentations of the day.

4. Class Discussion:

□ Invite students to investigate the sedimentary rock formed in our ocean of Jell-O.

□ What are their observations?

□ Where are the fruit pieces?

□ Where are the nuts?

□ Where are the crushed graham crackers?

□ Show them pictures of sedimentary rocks in your book.

□ Pass out a small portion of the sedimentary rock for all to enjoy!

□ Invite students to look more closely at rocks this week, especially as they complete 2-3 Activity A.

□ Encourage students to use their Science Journals as they explore rocks.

Observation Record

Activity B: Formation of Sedimentary Rocks

1) WEATHERING: Rocks breaking down into smaller pieces.

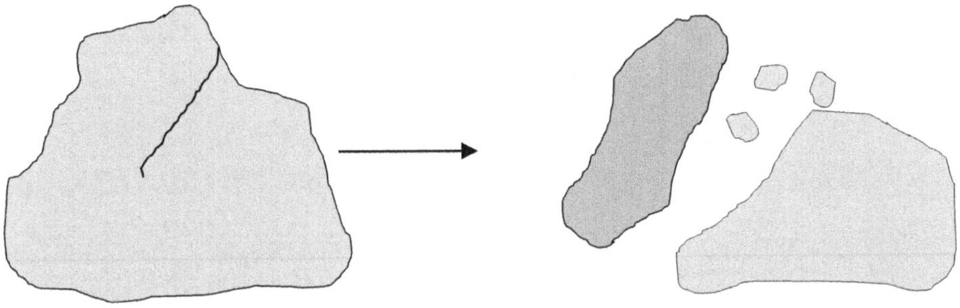

2) EROSION: Sediments (pieces of rocks, pebbles, sand and other debris transported to a body of water)

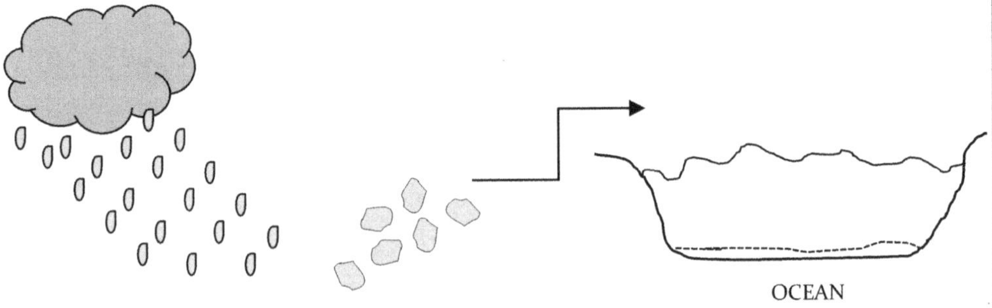

3) LITHIFICATION: Sediments are squeezed and bounded together due to pressure and dissolved minerals forming the layers of sedimentary rocks.

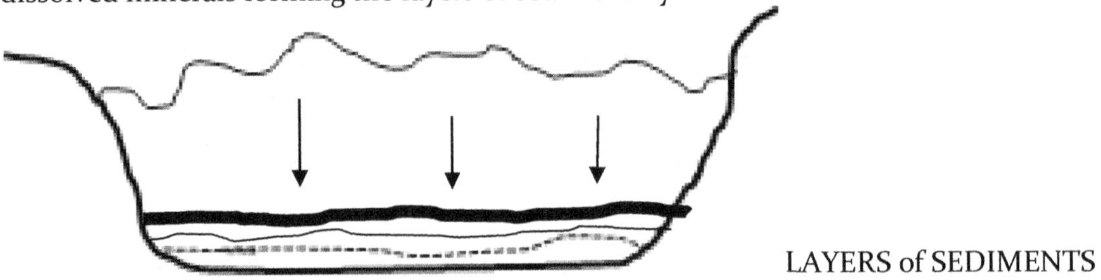

Unit 8: Erosion

- ☐ LESSON A: Observation and Discussion
    - Read the lesson carefully to make sure you have all needed supplies and you understand the content.
    - Observation Record: Draw what you observe from the activity. Color and label your picture.
- ☐ ACTIVITY A: Focus on Vocabulary
    - Draw what can happen (effect) based on the event that is shown on the left (cause).
- ☐ ACTIVITY B: Nature Journaling
    - Have your student draw the location where you went on a nature walk and any signs of weathering and/or erosion that you found.
- ☐ PARENT NOTES:

Lesson A: Erosion

Objective:

This lesson introduces students to erosion. Showing them how erosion helps change landscape.

Before the Lesson:

- ☐ Conduct science outside, whenever possible—check the lesson type and the weather.
- ☐ Gather and prep materials.

Materials Needed:

- ☐ 2 Clear plastic cups per student
- ☐ 2 Drinking straws per student
- ☐ 2 Cup of brown sugar per student
- ☐ ½ Cup of flour per student
- ☐ 1 Plastic plate per student (N.B. Any plate will work as long as its not paper)
- ☐ ½ Cup of water
- ☐ 3″ x 5″ Sheet of plastic saran wrap per student.
- ☐ 1 Sheet of paper or Science Journal per student
- ☐ 1 Set of colored pencils per student
- ☐ Pictures of sand castles

In Class:

1. Class Processing:
   - ☐ Ask students to share what they know about erosion.
   - ☐ Ask students if they have ever made a sand castle.
   - ☐ Allow students to describe their sand castles and how they made them.
   - ☐ Show students pictures of sand castles.
   - ☐ Then show students a sand castle after a wave has washed over it.
   - ☐ Invite students to look closely at the images. Ask students if they notice what happened to the sand castle.

 Explain that the sand castle was built by wet sand being pushed together through pressure to form a new shape. When the wave touched the sand, the particles that held it together began to break apart and therefore wash away.

2. Class Experiment

 Pass out clear plastic cups with ½ cup of brown sugar in them.

 Invite students to use their fingers to press down on the brown sugar creating pressure to form a sugar castle.

 Once the brown sugar has been compacted, carefully flip the cup on to the plate and gently squeeze the sides to release the sugar shape on to the plate.

*N.B. If the student did not create enough pressure, the sugar will fall into a big pile. To fix this problem simply place the sugar back into the cup and repeat the steps again until the sugar forms the cup shape on the plate.

 Invite students to look carefully at the sugar shape they just created.

 Ask students if they remember how rocks are formed.

 Tell students that the forming of the rocks requires pressure and the forming of the sugar castle requires pressure also.

 Have your students get out their Observation Record and draw the sugar castle using colored pencils.

 Once the drawing is done, pass out 1 straw per student.

 Ask students to try and change the shape of the sugar by blowing towards it, but not touching it. This represents how the wind can cause some erosion.

Have the students draw their observation after the wind erosion.

 Invite students to dip their fingers into the water and drip it on top of the sugar or pour a small amount onto the side of the sugar.

 Ask students "What do you think will happen if you use more water?"

 Ask students if they can think of an example of how water has helped shape the land around them.

 Invite students to record their findings on the paper or in their Observation Record.

 Pass out a second cup to students with a ½ cup of flour in each, and ask students to tap the flour gently to create a layer of plain four inside the cup.

 Invite students to cover the top of the cup with the clear saran wrap.

*N.B. You will want a tight coverage across the top.

 Next, show students how to poke a small hole in the saran wrap using a pencil.

 Ask students to look into the cup and share what the surface of the flour looks like.

 Tell students the flour represents the Earth, such as a dry sandy dessert. In some deserts the land is easily changed by the wind.

 Invite students to record what the flat flour looks like now on their sheet of paper

 Show students how to place the straw into their cup and blow the flour without touching it. Invite students to make a windy desert! After a few minutes, tell students to stop and look inside their cups. The flour will now be moved to valleys, mounds, or even deep holes.

 Explain that the wind, weather, and water are some of the ways the land around us is shaped and changed.

 Invite students to record their findings on their Observation Record.

3. Class Discussion:

 Encourage students to use their Science Journals as they look for examples of erosion this week.

Observation Record

Sugar castle

Before blowing	After blowing

Sugar castle

Before placing water	After placing water

Flour landscape

Before blowing	After blowing

Activity A: Cause and Effect of Erosion and Weathering

Weathering

CAUSE:
Water seeps in within the cracks of a boulder of rock when it rains. The water freezes during winter resulting to the widening of the cracks.

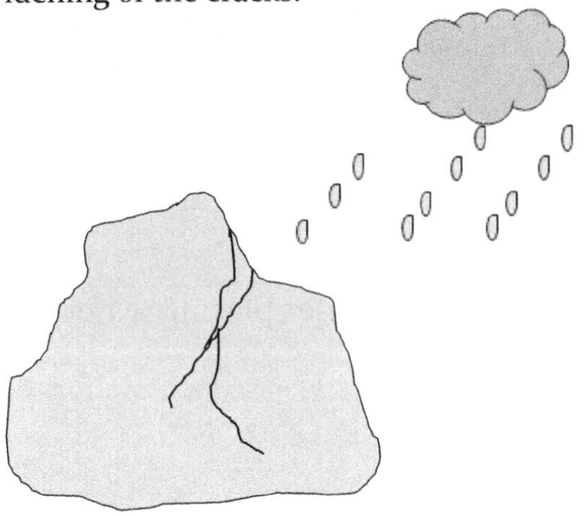

EFFECT:
As the cracks widen, it causes some pieces of the rocks to break apart.

Erosion

CAUSE:
During a big storm, beach sands are wash away by heavy winds and strong waves.

EFFECT:
The beach moved farther inland.

Activity B: My Nature Walk & Signs of Erosion

Date: ______________________________

Unit 9: Metamorphic Rocks

- ☐ LESSON A: Observation and Discussion
    - Read the lesson carefully to make sure you have all needed supplies and you understand the content.
    - Observation Record: Draw what you observe from the activity. Color and label your picture.
- ☐ ACTIVITY A: Nature Journaling
    - See Unit 5 Activity A for Rock Collecting Booklet. Complete the information for each METAMORPHIC rock that you collect.
- ☐ ACTIVITY B: Focus on Vocabulary
    - Determine if the description is true only for sedimentary rock, for metamorphic rock or for both.
    - Write the letter of the statement in the circle under sedimentary rock if it is true only for sedimentary rock.
    - Write the letter of the statement in the circle under metamorphic rock if it is true only for metamorphic rock.
    - Write the statement in the area where the circles overlap if the statement is true for both sedimentary and metamorphic rocks.
- ☐ ACTIVITY C: Nature Journaling
    - Have your student draw the location where you went on a nature walk and any rocks he or she found.

☐ PARENT NOTES:

Lesson A: Metamorphic Rocks

Objectives:

1) To identify different types of metamorphic rocks.
2) To compare and contrast different types of metamorphic rocks based in their physical appearance.
3) To help students understand the process involved in the formation of metamorphic rock.

Before the lesson:

- ☐ Conduct science outside, whenever possible—check the lesson type and the weather.
- ☐ Gather and prep materials.

Materials Needed:

- ☐ Slices of white and wheat bread
- ☐ Two to three types of cheese (one that melts easily and different color)
- ☐ One -two types of any cold cuts
- ☐ Sandwich press or iron
- ☐ Parchment paper if using iron.

In Class:

Class Processing:

3. Class Observation:
    - ☐ Ask students if they were able to find any metamorphic rocks when they were hunting for rocks last week.
    - ☐ Ask students to describe what a metamorphic rock looks like and to share anything they know about metamorphic rocks.
4. Class Processing:
    - ☐ Read or look at the pictures of the book about metamorphic rocks.
    - ☐ Show students a metamorphic rock and the corresponding parent rock where it was derived from e.g. quartzite from sand stone, marble from limestone, slate from shale.

- Talked about the word "Metamorphosis". Students would be familiar with this word from Cycle 1 during 'Life Cycle of Bugs'. Tell the students that the metamorphic rock was derived from a parent rock by undergoing changes or morphism due to extreme pressure and temperature. Just like the bug that undergo metamorphosis, a metamorphic rock underdo metamorphism resulting to a change in form from parent rock to metamorphic rock.
    - Parent rocks could be an igneous, sedimentary or another metamorphic rocks.

5. Class experiment:
    - Give each student two slices each of white and wheat bread, a slice of each type of cheese and cold cuts.
    - Ask the students to arrange the bread, cheese and cold cuts to make layered ham and cheese sandwich. Have the students draw the sedimentary rock sandwich they made in the Observation Record.
        - Tell the students that they made a sedimentary rock sandwich. This is a good time to review how sedimentary rocks are formed.
    - Tell the students that the sedimentary rock that they made will be changed into a metamorphic rock by subjecting it to high pressure and high temperature. Since the actual process of metamorphisms takes a very long time, we will fast forward the process by using a sandwich press. If press is not available, you can use an iron.
    - Place the sandwich in the sandwich press. Explain to the students that by pressing the sandwich in between two hot plates we are mimicking what would have happened underneath the earth's surface when metamorphism occur. If using an iron, wrap the sandwich with parchment paper and press using hot iron.
    - Cut the sandwich in half and observe the resulting layers.
    - Observe what happened to the sedimentary rock and draw your observation in the Observation Record.

Class Discussion:

- While students are journaling about their metamorphic rock sandwich, ask them how the resulting metamorphic rock differ from the parent sedimentary rock.

- How did the pressure and heat combined changed or transformed the sedimentary rock into a metamorphic rock? Did all of the sandwich filling melt or where there some layers that remain the same?
- Encourage the students to share any metamorphic rocks they have in their collection and describe their physical appearance.
- Remind the students that this is their last week to complete their rock collection and Rock Journal Notebook.

Observation Record

Sedimentary Rock Sandwich

High Temperature

High Pressure

Metamorphic Rock Sandwich

Activity B: Compare and Contrast using Venn Diagram

SEDIMENTARY ROCK

METAMORPHIC ROCK

BOTH

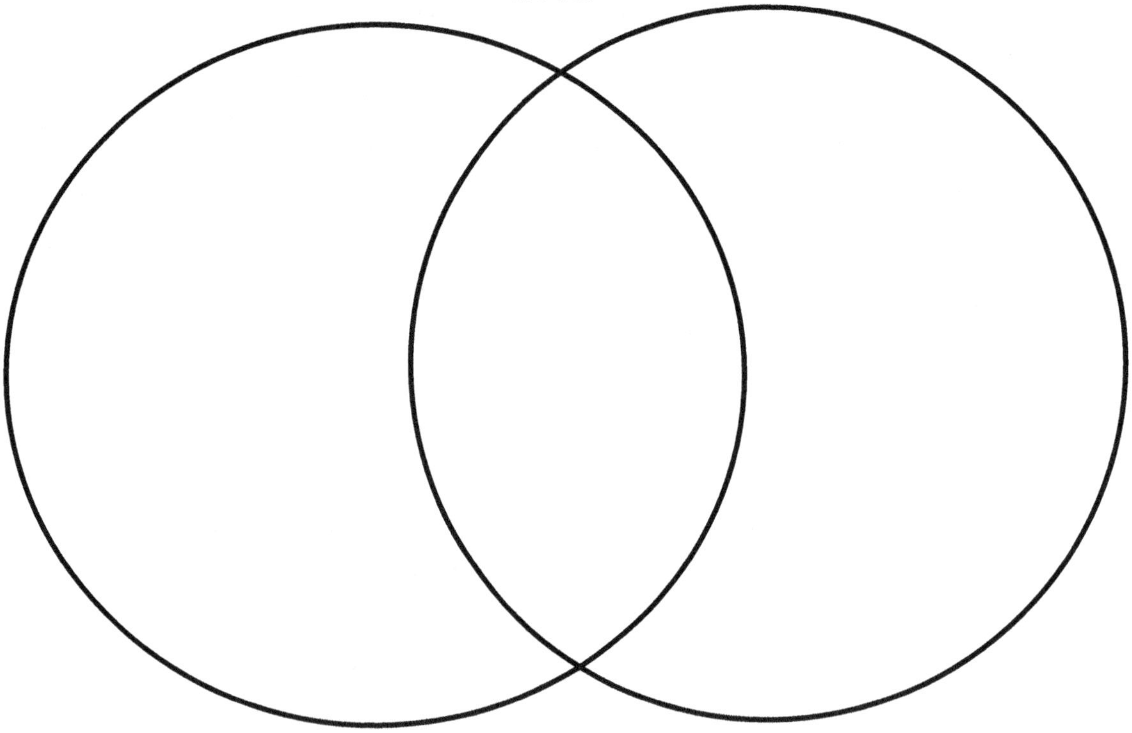

A. This rock is formed at or near Earth's surface.
B. This rock is formed with in the Earth's interior.
C. Contains minerals.
D. Contains fossils.
E. Undergo physical and chemical change during formation.
F. Formed due to high pressure and temperature.
G. Involves the process of sediment deposition and lithification.
H. Examples: Limestone, Sandstone, Shale
I. Examples: Marble, Quartzite, Slate

Activity C: My Nature Walk Observations

Date: ____

Unit 10: Testing Rocks & Minerals

- ☐ LESSON A: Observation and Discussion
  - Read the lesson carefully to make sure you have all needed supplies and you understand the content.
  - Observation Record: Help students record their observations.
- ☐ ACTIVITY A: Nature Journaling
  - Go on a walk in the woods or beach and collect 1-2 rocks that look differently. Fill in the information sheets below. Draw your observation inside each box.
- ☐ ACTIVITY B: Focus on Vocabulary
  - Using the rock information from Activity A, help your student dictate or write a poem about his or her rock. Illustrate the poem with your student.
- ☐ ACTIVITY C: Nature Journaling
  - Have your student draw the location where you went on a nature walk and any rocks he or she found.
- ☐ PARENT NOTES:

____

____

____

____

____

____

____

____

Lesson A: Testing Rocks & Minerals

Objectives:

1. To determine the hardness of different rocks and minerals using common house tools.
2. To be familiar with Moh's hardness scale

Before the Co-op Meeting:

- ☐ Conduct science outside, whenever possible—check the lesson type and the weather.
- ☐ Gather rocks for the students that you have tested and pre-identified.
- ☐ Gather and prep all materials.

Materials Needed:

☐ 4-6 rocks and/or minerals *if using rocks, pick rocks that are smooth and not grainy; assign

a letter for each rock and/or mineral starting from A and so on.

☐ (1-3) copper pennies (3.5 hardness)

☐ (1) knife or glass plate (5.5 hardness)

☐ (1) steel nail or steel file (6.5 hardness)

☐ (1) drill bit (8.5 hardness)

In Class:

1. Class Observation:

   ☐ Have the students sit in a semi-circle in front of you outside.

   ☐ Show them several rocks that look very different from the each other.

   ☐ Explain that there are tests that we can perform to identify rocks that are different.

   ☐ Show them a soft rock and a hard rock (without pointing that out!).

   ☐ Pass these two rocks around and ask students if they can tell a difference between the two rocks.

   ☐ What did they discover? (one is hard and the other is soft)

☐ Explain that there is something called "Mohs Hardness Scale" which allows us to group rocks in ranges by hardness and softness.

☐ Show them several more rocks and see if they can put them in order by hardness (keep the order for later in the lesson).

To help your student to determine the hardness of the rock samples you have, you can show them that if they scratch two rocks together, sometimes one rock can get scratch.

Which rock is harder? The one that scratched or the one that got scratched?

What if the rocks did not get scratched at all? What does it mean?

Record the ordering they made from softest to hardest in the Observation Record.

☐ Now, explain to students that the hardness of rocks and minerals can be determine using the Mohs Hardness Scale Test that goes from 1-10, 1 being the softest and 10 being the hardest (diamonds!). The Mohs test is a qualitative scale to determine the scratch resistance of different minerals using one sample of natural mineral at a time to scratch another mineral.

☐ Ask students to feel their own fingernails.

☐ Ask students how hard they think their fingernails are on a scale from 1-10.

☐ Tell the students that most fingernails are rated 2.5 on the Mohs Hardness Scale. WOW! That is not very hard!

☐ Show students the copper pennies. Have them guess how much harder or softer they are than fingernails.

☐ Explain that copper pennies are 3.5!

☐ Continue this process of question- explanation with the glass plate/knife (5.5), steel nail/file (6.5), and drill bit (8.5).

2. Class Experiment:

   ☐ Ask the students to test each rock or mineral that you provided in class using the common house objects that have known hardness. Using the ordering they made initially, test the rocks/minerals. In their Observation Record, place a check mark for each corresponding rock that was scratched by each material of known hardness (fingernails, copper pennies, knife and so on).

   *Take note of the guideline for testing Mohs Hardness for rocks and minerals

3. Class Processing:

- Show students their line of ordered rocks again. Using the results of the testing done by using materials of known hardness, do they need to re-order or re-arrange the rocks/minerals?

- How to interpret your results:

  * For example, if Rock A was scratched by fingernails, it means that Rock A has a Mohs Hardness of less than 2.5

  If Rock C was scratched by copper pennies but not scratched by fingernails, Rock C has a Mohs Hardness between 2.5 and 3.5, and that Rock C is harder than Rock A.

  If Rock B was scratched by steel nail/file but not scratched by fingernails, copper pennies or knife, Rock B has a Mohs hardness between 5.5 and 6.5; and that Rock B is harder than Rocks A and C.

  To arrange the rocks from softest to hardest, the order is Rock A, C, B.

4. Class Discussion:

   - Now tell students that diamonds are rated as 10 on the Mohs Hardness Scale.
   - Can they imagine why you did not bring diamonds to class?
   - Ask students if they had ever thought about how hard or soft rocks are before.
   - Encourage them to go home and find rocks to categorize by hardness this week.

Guideline for Testing Moh's Hardness in Rocks and Minerals

- ✓ Use the smooth and unscratched surface of the rock or mineral of your test specimen.
- ✓ Place the test rock or mineral specimen on a stable surface and hold it firmly exposing the smooth surface to be tested.
- ✓ Hold one of the standard hardness specimen in the other hand and place a point of that specimen against the selected flat surface of the rock or mineral specimen.
- ✓ Firmly press and drag the point of the standard specimen across the surface of the unknown specimen.
- ✓ After scratching, examine the surface of the unknown rock or mineral specimen. Using your finger, brush away any mineral fragments or powder that was produced. Did the test produce a scratch? Be careful not to confuse mineral powder or residue with a scratch. A scratch will be a distinct groove cut in the mineral surface, not a mark on the surface that wipes away.
- ✓ Conduct the test a second time to confirm your results.

Observation Record

Rock ordering I. Arrange the rock/mineral samples from softest to hardest and write the letter of the rock/mineral in each box in the order of softest to hardest.

SOFTEST ⟶ HARDEST

Mohs Hardness Scale. Place a check-mark if the rock was scratched using the following materials.

ROCKS	Finger nail (2.5)	Copper Penny (3.5)	Glass plate/knife (5.5)	Steel nail/ Steel file (6.5)	Drill Bit (8.5)
A					
B					
C					
D					
E					
F					

Rock Re-Ordering II. Arrange the rock/mineral samples from softest to hardest using the result from the table above, and write the letter of the rock/mineral in each box in the order of softest to hardest.

SOFTEST ⟶ HARDEST

1) Which of your rock or mineral sample is the softest? ____________________
2) Which of your rock or mineral sample is the hardest? ____________________
3) Are there any rock or minerals that have the same hardness? If yes, which one?

____

Activity A: Properties of Rocks

Draw your rock.	What is the texture of your rock? Smooth or Rough (Grainy)?	Is it shiny or dull?
Drop your rock in a cup of water. Did it float or sink?	Drop your rock in vinegar and leave it there for 2 minutes. Did it form fizz or bubbles?	Is it attracted to magnet or not?

Activity B: My Rock Poem

Unit 11: Landforms

- ☐ LESSON A: Observation and Discussion
    - o Read the lesson carefully to make sure you have all needed supplies and you understand the content.
    - o Observation Record: Cut the names and definitions of different landforms and glue them to the correct landforms found in the picture.
- ☐ ACTIVITY A: Focus on Vocabulary
    - o Figure out the word in the middle by filling in the different landforms across using the clues provided.
- ☐ ACTIVITY B: Nature Journaling
    - o Have your student draw the location where you went on a nature walk and any landforms and/or body of water he or she observed.
- ☐ PARENT NOTES:

____

____

____

____

____

____

____

____

____

Lesson A: Vocabulary and Draw Landforms

Objectives:

1. To learn the different types of landforms.
2. To be able to look at a map and identify the different landforms.

Before the Lesson:

2. Conduct science outside, whenever possible—check the lesson type and the weather.

3. Gather and prep all materials.

Materials Needed:

- □ Set of colored pencils or crayons per student
- □ Scissors per student
- □ Glue stick per student
- □ (1) Observation Record: "Picture Vocabulary Landforms" per student

In Class:

1. Class Observation:

□ Have the students sit in a semi-circle in front of you outside.

□ Show them a topographic map. You can use any topographic map or you can visit the USGS link below to print one.

https://www.usgs.gov/core-science-systems/ngp/tnm-delivery/maps

□ Explain that a map is a small-scale picture of a location. Spend some time looking at the map and talking about what they see.

- Help students identify mountains, plains, valleys, hills.
- How do we know where the mountains are? How they are represented in the map (contour lines). The closer the lines are in the contour the steeper the mountain is.
- Can they also identify some bodies of water? Usually bodies of water are colored blue.

2. Class Processing:

    □ Cut the names and definitions of the different land forms (Observation Record)

    □ Say one landform vocabulary word out loud.

    □ Read the description of the landform.

    □ Look at the Observation Record and see if your students can find an example of that landform on the drawn landscape.

    □ Glue the name and definition on the drawn landscape as you go through the various landforms.

Observation Record: Landforms and Bodies of Water

OCEAN- The large body of salt water. Covers ¾ of Earth's surface.

PENINSULA- A piece of land that extends into the body of water and is surrounded on three sides.

ISLAND- An area of land completely surrounded by water

HILL- An old mountain which because of erosion has become rounder and shorter.

MOUNTAIN- A high, rocky land, usually with steep sides and a pointed or rounded top, higher than a hill

DELTA- A low-lying area where sediments are deposited from the river mouth to another body of water ocean or sea.

VALLEY- A low land between hills or mountains.

PLATEAU- A flat highland area with steep sides; an elevated plain

RIVER- A large stream of water flowing through the land into a lake or ocean.

BAY- A salt body of water that reaches into land; smaller than a Gulf.

PLAIN- A broad, flat gently sloping area. Usually with low elevation

LAKE- A large body of water surrounded by land.

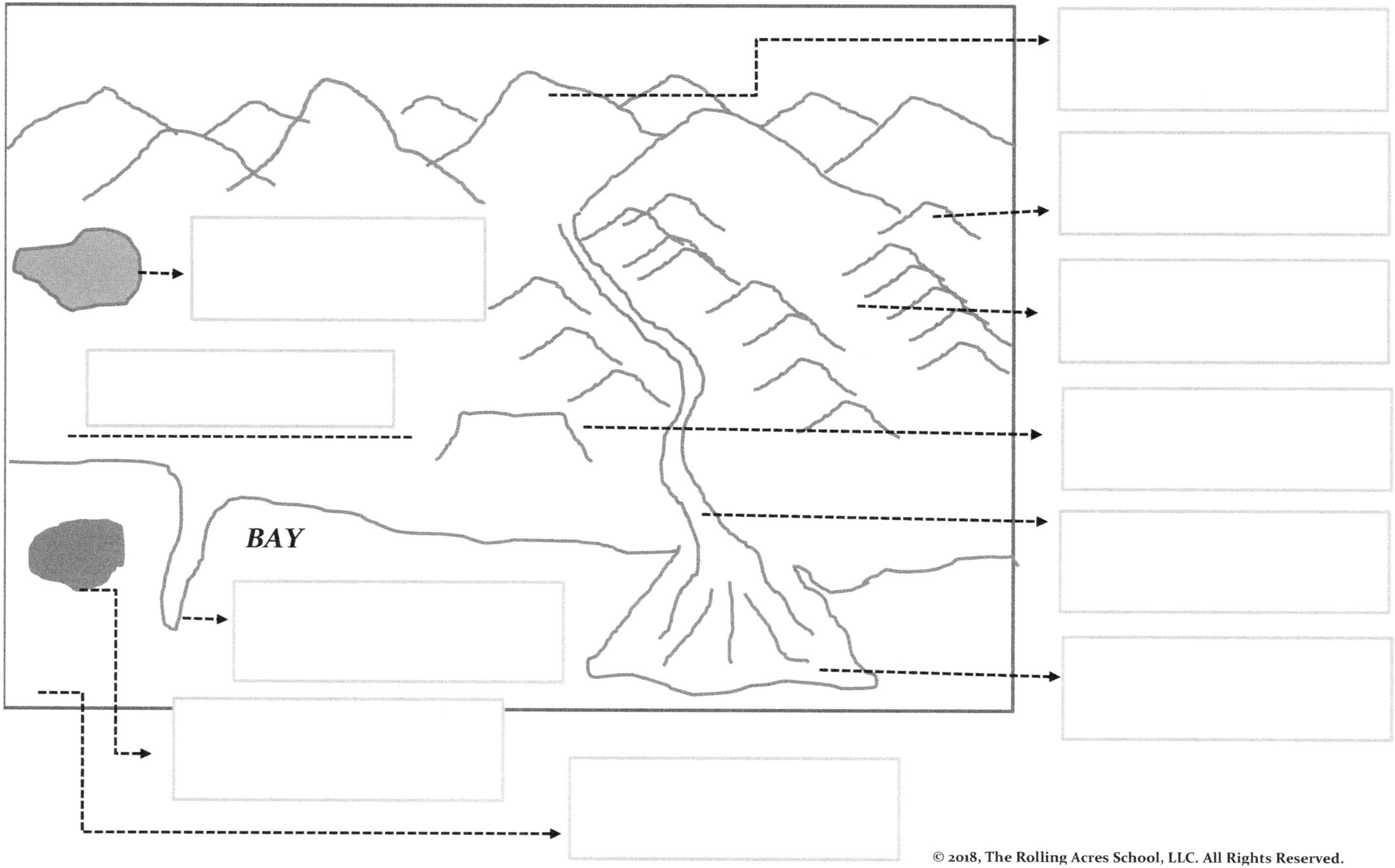
BAY

Activity A: Landforms Word Puzzle

	1	___ ___ ___
___ ___	2	___ ___
	3	
___ ___ ___ ___	4	___
	F	___ ___ ___ ___
	5	___ ___ ___ ___
	6	___ ___ ___ ___
	7	___ ___ ___ ___ ___ ___ ___
___ ___ ___ ___ ___	8	___ ___ ___

Clues:

1) A large body of water completely surrounded by land.
2) A broad, flat or gently rolling area; usually low in elevation.
3) An area of land completely surrounded by water.
4) A low-lying area where sediments are deposited from the river mouth to another body of water such as lake, ocean or sea.
5) The largest body of salt water; these cover 3/4 of the earth's surface.
6) A large stream of water flowing through the land into a lake, ocean, or other body of water.
7) A high, rocky land, usually with steep sides and a pointed or rounded top, higher than a hill.
8) A piece of land that extends into a body of water and is surrounded on three sides by water.

Information for terms and definitions found at:
http://worldlandforms.com/landforms/list-of-all-landforms

Activity B: Finding Landforms

Date: ____

Unit 12: Soil

- ☐ LESSON A: Observation and Discussion
    - Read the lesson carefully to make sure you have all needed supplies and you understand the content.
    - Observation Record: Draw and color your soil profile cereal treat.
- ☐ ACTIVITY A: Focus on Vocabulary
    - Using newspaper or magazines, find pictures that can represent the different functions or importance of soil. Cut and paste them around using the spider diagram. If you need more space you can copy and paste the spider diagram on a bigger paper to make a poster with your picture collage. You can also draw your own picture.
- ☐ ACTIVITY B: Nature Journaling
    - Go on a nature walk (beach/sandy area, marsh/clay soil area, or the woods) and compare the type of substrate you can find in those locations to your garden soil.
    - Compare the soils/substrate in the location you visited and your own yard in terms of color, texture and the types of plants that grow in each area.
- ☐ PARENT NOTES:

Lesson A: Soil Profile

Objectives:

3. To observe and identify the different layers of soil.
4. To learn the different components of soil.
5. To discuss the importance of top soil in vegetation.

Before the Lesson:

- ☐ Conduct science outside, whenever possible—check the lesson type and the weather.
- ☐ Gather and prep all materials.

Materials Needed:

- ☐ Three types of cereal to represent the different layers of the soil (bedrock, subsoil, topsoil and the organic components)
- ☐ Clear plastic cup or glass
- ☐ Milk
- ☐ Spoon
- ☐ Soil Profile Observation Record
- ☐ Actual soil profile (if available). You can obtain a soil profile by digging a hole in your yard. You can use this to observe the different layers as you dig.

In Class:

1. Class Observation:
   - ☐ Ask students to share what they know about soil.
   - ☐ Ask students if they have ever made a mud pie or planted a garden.
   - ☐ Allow students to describe how they have used soil.
   - ☐ Tell the students that you will pick a spot in a yard to dig and as you dig, you will try to observe how the color, texture and other components of the soil changes as you dig deeper. If digging is not possible, you can use the Soil Profile Observation Record in the discussion.

- Using the Soil Profile Observation Record, compare the actual layers of the soil you are digging with the picture and discuss the color, texture, thickness and other components they observe for each layer.

2. Class Activity:

   - Tell the students that they will recreate the soil profile using different types of cereal that they can enjoy after the activity.

   a. First present to students three to four different types of cereal and ask them which one looks like the bed rock, the sub-soil, the top soil and the organic layer. Cereal for bed rocks would be chunkier and lighter in color to represent bigger rocks. Cereal for sub-soil can be similar to the bed rock but crushed to a finer texture. Light color cereal would represent lesser organic materials and more minerals. The cereal for top soil should be darker (chocolate cereal that has been crushed) to represent rich organic matter. You can add another layer for humus which includes leaf litter, dead plants, insects and other microorganisms. This is normally above and darker than the top soil.

   b. Compare your cereal profile with an actual soil profile. Draw your cereal profile using the Observation Record.

   c. Tell the students that soil also contains moisture and air space. To demonstrate how soil contains about 25% airspace, use a similar cup that you used to make the cereal soil profile and fill it with milk the same height as the cereal soil. Slowly pour the milk into the cereal soil profile. Ask the students to observe for air bubbles as they pour the milk slowly. Stop pouring milk when it reached the top part of the cereal. Explain to the students that the air in soil was displaced by the milk that they poured in.

   d. How much milk was used to fill in the air space? It should be close to ¼ or 1/3 of the total amount of milk in the cup.

   e. After the activity give students plastic spoons to enjoy their cereal soil profile treat.

3. Class processing:

   - Encourage students to use their Science Journals as they look for examples of how soil is used this week.

Observation Record

SOIL PROFILE

CEREAL SOIL PROFILE

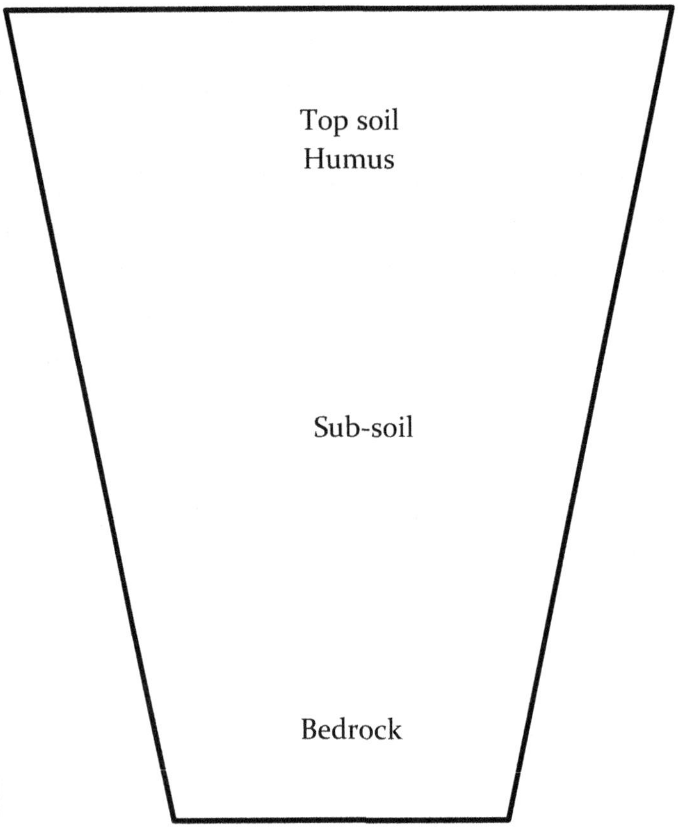

Activity A: Spider Diagram

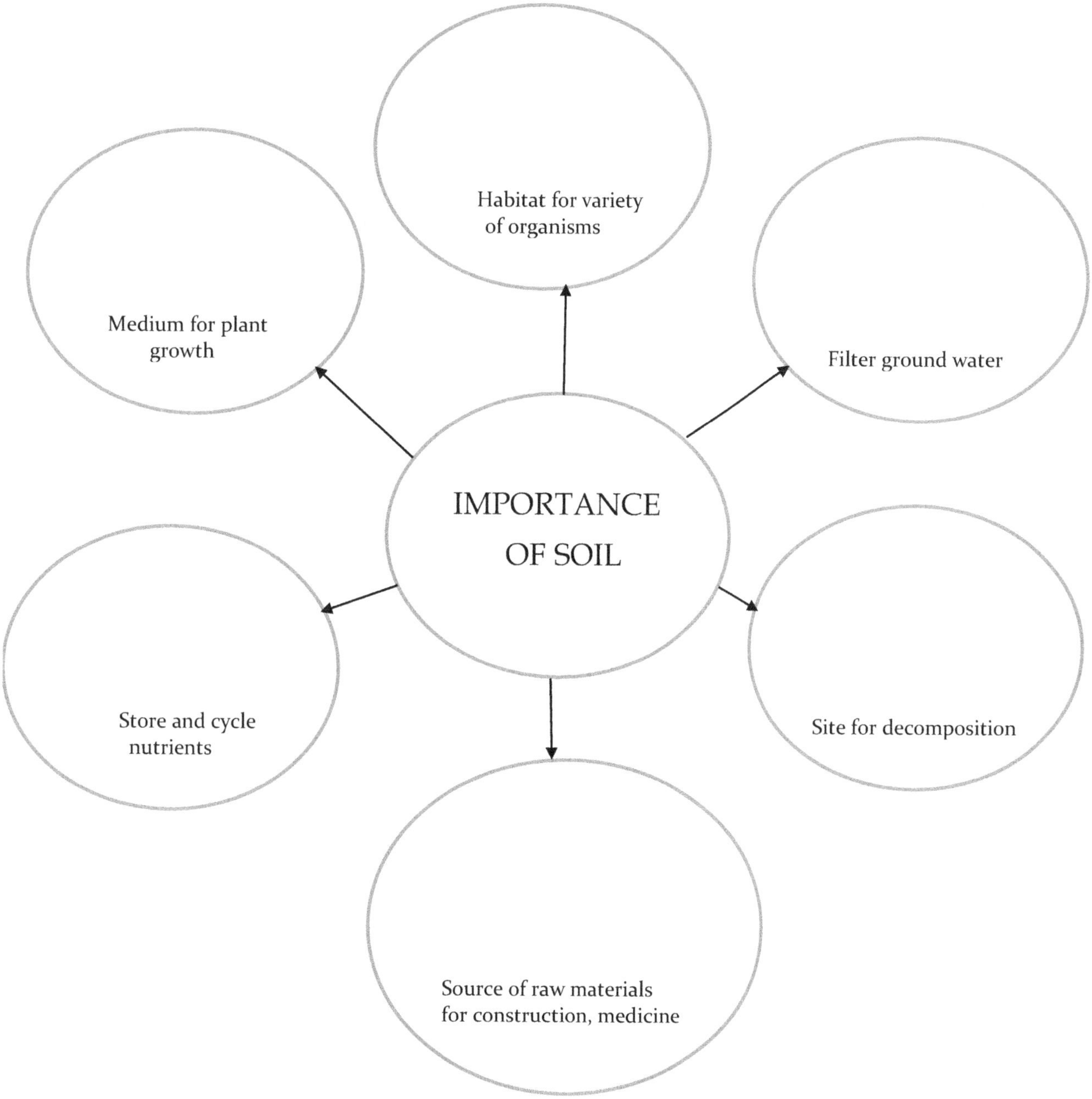

Activity B: My Nature Walk and Soil Types

Date: ______________________________

Unit 13: Compost, Recycle, Reuse

- ☐ LESSON A: Observation and Discussion
  - Read the lesson carefully to make sure you have all needed supplies and you understand the content.
  - Observation Record: Fill in the log to help you sort out materials used and leftover from lunch. Put a check mark (/) under Reuse, Recycle or Compost and fill in the information on ways to reuse the material. If any of the material cannot be categorized as Reuse, Recycle or Compost, it is considered Trash and fill in ways that can be used as an alternative material to reduce the trash production.
- ☐ ACTIVITY A: Putting an Idea into Action
  - Pick any material/s from your reuse bin and think of ways to use it in a new way. Draw how you reused the material/s below.
- ☐ ACTIVITY B: Nature Journaling
  - Gather the materials for your composting project. We will be using materials that you've been sorting into reuse, recycle and compost bins.

1. Observation Record: Record each week the changes that you observe inside the compost bottle.

- ☐ PARENT NOTES:

____

____

____

____

____

____

Lesson A: Compost, Recycle, Reuse

Objectives:

1. To introduce students to composting, recycling, and reusing household items.
2. To sort and determine materials for recycling, reusing and composting.
3. To discuss the importance of composting, recycling, and reusing.

Before the Lesson:

- Conduct science outside, whenever possible—check the lesson type and the weather.
- Gather and prep all materials.

Materials Needed:

- ☐ Any packages or materials used in making and eating lunch
- ☐ Any leftover food from lunch
- ☐ Observation Record "Lunch Packages and Leftover Log"

In Class:

4. Class Observation:

☐ Ask students if they know where the packages of food we buy goes after using them. How about the leftover food?

☐ Look at a food packaging and discuss how the package was made. What are the resources that were used to make the packaging?

☐ Introduce the idea of reuse, recycle and compost.

Reuse: Finding new uses to the materials you already have instead of buying a new one.

Recycle: For materials that cannot be reused, they can be used as raw materials to make new products. A wide variety of different materials can be recycled, including paper, plastic, glass, and metal.

Composting: Is a natural way of decomposition of organic materials (biodegradable) into rich soil. Composting is one way to reduce waste.

☐ Tell the students that as God's steward of His creation, we have to use the resources He has given us properly and wisely. Being mindful of how we use things and reducing our daily household waste is one way of taking care of our world that God created.

5. Class Activity:

   . Lay out all the packages used in making your lunch, and leftover food and scraps.

   a. Using Observation Record, list all the materials that you are going to sort.

   b. Asked the students to categorize each material to something that can be reuse, recycle or place in the compost pile.

6. Class processing:

   - Have the student do this exercise for 2-3 times and see if they can categorize materials on their own.
   - If you don't have any recycling or reuse bins, get two plastic bins or boxes and label them REUSE, and RECYLE. Use a plastic container or bowl for food scraps that can be composted.
   - Have the students placed the materials they sorted in their respective bins or containers.
   - Are there any materials that cannot be categorize as Reuse, Recycle or Compost? If any of the material is categorized as waste or trash, discuss ways on how we can reduce the waste production or what alternative materials that can be use instead to reduce waste.
     Example: Individual juice box- instead of buying individual juice boxes, families can get juice in bigger containers that can be placed in individual reusable bottles made of glass or plastic. The gallon juice containers can also be reuse or recyle after use.

Observation Record: Lunch Packages and Leftover Log

Material	Reuse	Ways to reuse the material	Recycle	Compost	Trash	Alternative practice or material
Example: *½ Gal juice bottle*	/	*Use as bird feeder, use as planter*	/			

Material	Reuse	Ways to reuse the material	Recycle	Compost	Trash	Alternative practice or material
Example: *Paper plate*					/	*Use of plates that can be washed and reused.*

Activity A: My Reuse Project

Activity B: Reuse, Recycle and Compost Project

From your Reuse or Recycle bin: Two 2L or 3L soda bottle with cap, newspaper or paper scrap, piece of cloth.

From your compost bin: Collected vegetable and fruit scraps, used ground coffee beans, egg shells etc.

Other materials: scissors, rubber band, duct tape, ruler, permanent marker.

Procedure:

A) Compost Bottle Column

a. Cut one bottle two inches below from the neck and the other bottle 2 inches from the bottom.

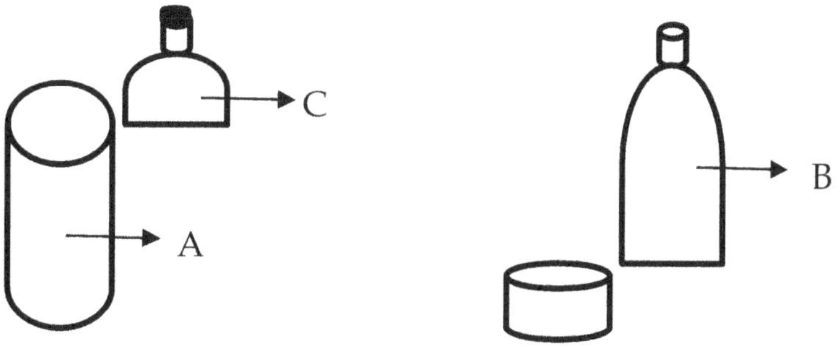

b. Wrap the opening of 'B' with a square piece of cloth and secure using a rubber band. Poke holes around 'B' using nails, then place the 'B' upside down into 'A'.

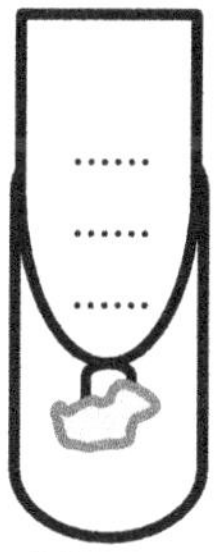

c. Fill in the plastic column with organic materials. First, place a cupful or two of soil then layer it with food scraps, then with dried leaves or grass clippings, then with shredded newspaper putting soil in between each layer. You can repeat these layers ending with soil making sure you leave at least an inch from the edge of the container.
Spray some water making sure that the piles are moist but not too wet. Cover the pile using 'C' with cap. Secure the different parts of the column using duct tape. Mark the uppermost layer of the pile so that changes in the volume can be observed as the materials inside decompose. Place the compost bottle next to a light (windowsill) and make sure to add water inside if it started to

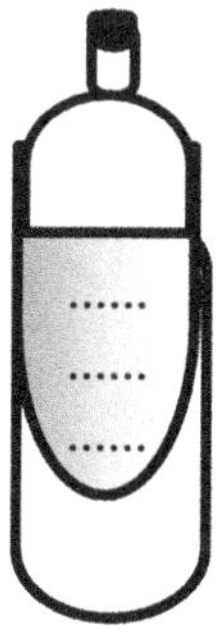

Dry up. Signs of decomposition should be visible within 3-4 weeks.

Observation Record

WEEK	Description of each layers	Height of the whole pile
1	Food scrap- Shredded paper- Grass clippings/leaves-	
2	Food scrap- Shredded paper- Grass clippings/leaves-	
3	Food scrap- Shredded paper- Grass clippings/leaves-	
4	Food scrap- Shredded paper- Grass clippings/leaves-	

Unit 14: Review

- ☐ LESSON A: Review
    - Complete the review with your student.
    - Make sure all assignments in Units 1-13 were completed. These are great weeks for getting caught up and organized before starting the second half of the workbook.
- ☐ PARENT NOTES: Make any notes about the first half. How did your student do? What could you help him or her with more, so he or she is interested and invested? How could you challenge your student more? Now is a great time to adjust for a great second half of the year!

Lesson A: Review

Unit 1. Layers of the Earth

Draw the four layers of the Earth and label the layers (Inner Core, Outer Core, Mantle, and Crust)

Units 2-4 Mountains, Volcanoes, Earthquakes

Matching type. Write the correct letter of the description of the types of mountains, volcanoes and earthquakes.

_______ 1) Faut-Block mountain

_______ 2) Fold mountain

_______ 3) Dome mountain

_______ 4) Volcanic mountain

_______ 5) Plateu

_______ 6) Shield volcano

______ 7) Strato or composite volcano

______ 8) Cindercone volcano

______9) S wave

______ 10) P wave

A) The fastest and first wave to travel during earthquake.

B) A slower wave that can not pass through parts of the core during earthquake.

C) Volcano that is broad and gently sloping.

D) Volcano that is typically steep-sided, symmetircal and has alternating layer of lava flow.

E) The simplest type of volcano with only one vent.

F) This type of mountain has been worn down due to erosion.

G) This type of mountain is formed when the magma underneath pushed some weak parts of the crust and magma seeps out, or erupts to the surface.

H) This type of mountain is formed when parts of the Earth's crust along fault lines tilt and lift up as the crusts move.

I) This type of mountain is formed when the magma underneath pushed some weak parts of the crust without breaking through the surface.

J) This type of mountain is formed when two plates collide and press each other that result to some of the tallest mountains around.

Units 5-10 Rocks

Complete the Rock Cycle using the terms below.

A) Igneous Rocks, B) Metamorphic Rocks, C) Weathering-Erosion, D)Deposition-Lithification, E)Cooling, F)Melting

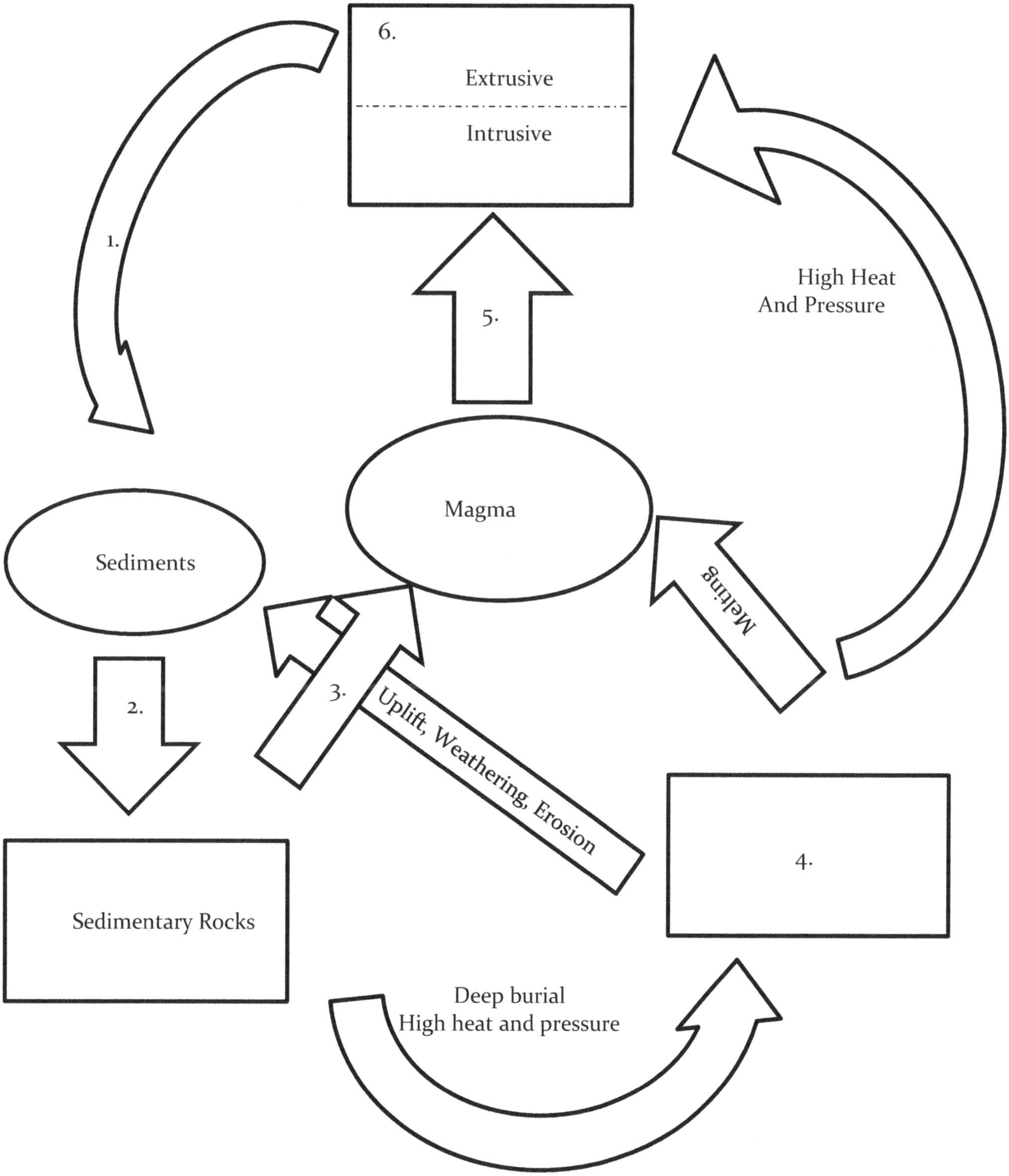

Unit 11. Landforms and Bodies of Water

Identification. Pick from the terms inside the box to identify the landform or body of water being described.

Delta	Hill	Island	Lake
Mountain	Ocean	Peninsula	
Plain	River	Valley	

__________________ 1) A large body of water completely surrounded by land.

__________________ 2) The largest body of salt water; these cover 3/4 of the earth's surface.

__________________ 3) A large stream of water flowing through the land into a lake, ocean, or other body of water.

__________________ 4) A broad, flat or gently rolling area; usually low in elevation.

__________________ 5) An area of land completely surrounded by water.

__________________ 6) A low-lying area where sediments are deposited from the river mouth to another body of water such as lake, ocean or sea.

__________________ 7) An old mountain which because of erosion has become rounder and shorter.

__________________ 8) A low land between hills or mountains.

__________________ 9) A high, rocky land, usually with steep sides and a pointed or rounded top, higher than a hill.

__________________ 10) A piece of land that extends into a body of water and is surrounded on three sides by water.

Unit 15: Review

- ☐ LESSON A: Review Memory Work
    - o Complete the review with your student.
- ☐ PARENT NOTES: Make any notes about the first half. How did your student do? What could you help him or her with more, so he or she is interested and invested? How could you challenge your student more? Now is a great time to adjust for a great second half of the year!

Lesson A: Review Memory Work

UNIT 1

Q: What are the four layers of the earth?

A: Crust, Mantle, Outer Core, Inner Core

UNIT 2

Q: What are five types of mountains?

A: Fold, Fault-block, Dome, Volcanic, Plateau

UNIT 3

Q: What are the three main types of volcanoes?

A: Shield, Cinder Cone, Composite/Stratovolcano

UNIT 5

Q: What are the three types of rocks?

A: Igneous, Sedimentary, Metamorphic

UNIT 6

Q: What are some types of igneous rocks?

A: Granite, Pumice, Obsidian, Basalt

UNIT 7

Q: What are some types of sedimentary rocks?

A: Limestone, Shale, Conglomerate, Chert, Sandstone

UNIT 9

Q: What are some types of metamorphic rocks?

A: Slate, Schist, Marble, Gneiss

UNIT 10

Q: What are some tests geologists use to identify minerals in rocks?

A: Color, Luster, Streak Test, Acid Test, Moh's Hardness Test

UNIT 11

Q: What are some common landforms and waterforms?

A: Peninsula, Gulf, Cape, Bay, Isthmus, Strait

Unit 16: Plant Growth and Compost

- ☐ LESSON A: Observation and Discussion
    - Read the lesson carefully to make sure you have all needed supplies and you understand the content.
    - Common Decomposers
- ☐ ACTIVITY A: Nature Journaling
    - Observe the growth of your seeds at different types of growth media. Measure in centimeters (cm) plant growth and record any additional changes that you can observe for at least a week.
- ☐ ACTIVITY B: Focus on Vocabulary
    - Find out the missing words to complete each sentence by using the code.
- ☐ PARENT NOTES:

Lesson A: Plant Growth Experiment Using Compost

Objectives:

To compare the germination and growth of plants in various amount of compost.

Before the Lesson:

2. Conduct science outside, whenever possible—check the lesson type and the weather.

3. Gather and prep all materials.

Materials Needed:

- ☐ Planting trays (with at least 6 compartments) or reuse similar plastic containers
- ☐ Compost (from Unit 13)
- ☐ Yard soil (not potting soil)
- ☐ Fast germinating seeds (beans and peas, radishes, squash, pumpkins, marigolds)
- ☐ Lights source (Natural or artificial)
- ☐ Ruler for plant growth measurement.

In Class:

1. Class Observation:

   ☐ Tell the students that they will grow plants from seeds using the compost that they made from Unit 13.

   ☐ Ask the students what are the changes they observed inside their compost bottle for four weeks. Can they still see the thing they put in there or did they look different now? Are there any organisms that live in their compost? You can dump the compost on a tray and look for organisms if there are any.

   ☐ Review the process of decomposition and how different organisms help in the break-down of organic materials back to their simpler forms.

   Example: When leaves fall, decomposers such as worms eat dead leaves then passes it out as 'cast'. The cast or waste of an earthworm can now be easily consumed by bacteria which then further breaks down organic materials into their simplest form like nutrients.

- Look at "Decomposers in our Garden", and have students read the different organism that aid in decomposition process. For older students you can differentiate 'Decomposers' vs 'Detrivores'.
    - ❖ Decomposers are organisms that break down dead plants and animals, and wastes of other organisms e.g. bacteria and fungi (mushrooms).
    - ❖ Detrivores are animals that consume and break down dead organic material and excrete nutrients back into the ecosystem e.g. earthworms, slugs, snails, spiders, ants, mites, millipede, and centipede.
- Remind the students that the compost they made is very high in nutrients as the decomposers present in the soil have broken down any organic materials that they placed in their compost column like the grass clippings, fruit and vegetables peels, paper etc. into their simpler forms that the plants can now use and absorb as the plants grow.

2. Class Activity:
    - Fill two-three compartments of the tray with 100% compost, two-three compartments with 50% soil:50% compost, and the other two-three compartments with 100% soil.
    - Placed three seeds in each compartments and water after planting.
    - Placed the planting tray next to window sill or any area in the house where it can get at least 6 hours of sun. You can also use artificial light such as lamp as source of light.
    - Fill Activity A Observation Log for plant growth.
3. Class processing:
    - Ask the students in which growth medium will the seeds germinate first? In which growth medium will the plant grow faster after germination?

Observation Record: "Decomposers" (Detrivores) in our Garden

The following organisms are examples of decomposers that help break down organic materials in our soil back to their simpler forms (nutrients). Decomposers help 'digest' food scraps in the compost column into compost.

EARTHWORM

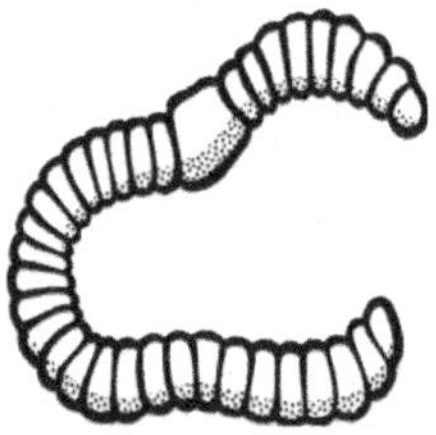

SLUG

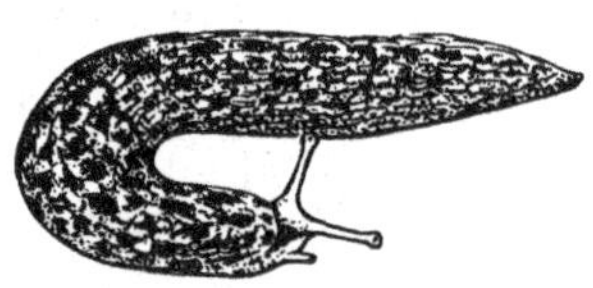

SPRINGTAIL

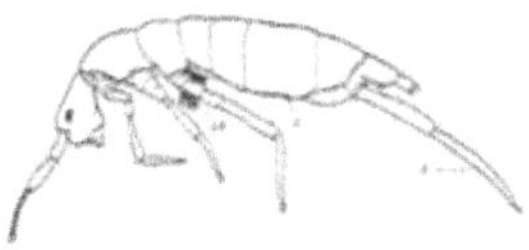

SNAIL

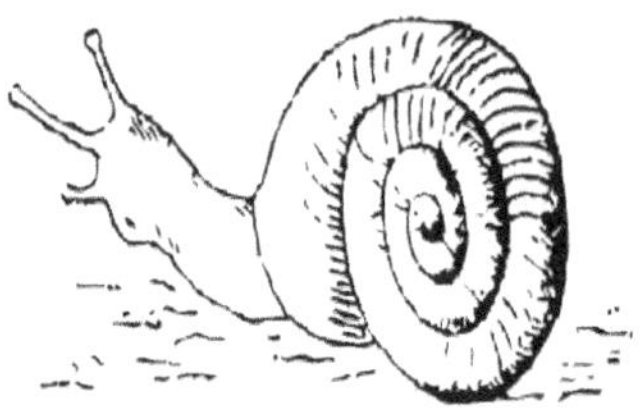

BEETLE

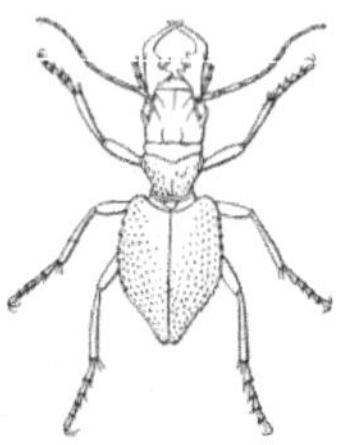

ANT

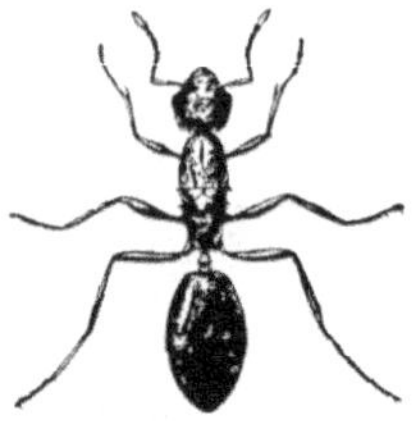

CENTIPEDE

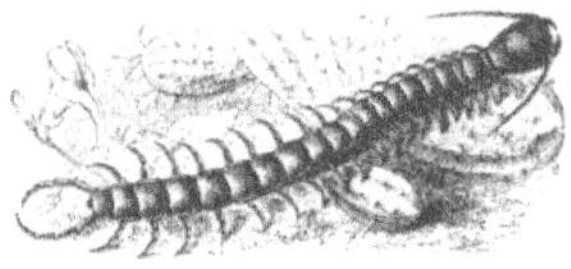

MILLIPEDE

Images from: https://publicdomainvectors.org, https://www.pdclipart.org, https://openclipart.org

Activity A: Observation Log Plant Growth

DAY		# of Seeds that Germinated	# of Stem/s	Ave. Height of Stem/s (cm)	Total # of Leaves	Other notes:
1	100%soil					
	50%:50%					
	100%compost					
2	100%soil					
	50%:50%					
	100%compost					
3	100%soil					
	50%:50%					
	100%compost					
4	100%soil					
	50%:50%					
	100%compost					
5	100%soil					
	50%:50%					
	100%compost					
6	100%soil					
	50%:50%					
	100%compost					
7	100%soil					
	50%:50%					
	100%compost					

Draw your plants after a week of growth in 100% Soil, 50%Soils:50%Compost, and 100% Compost.

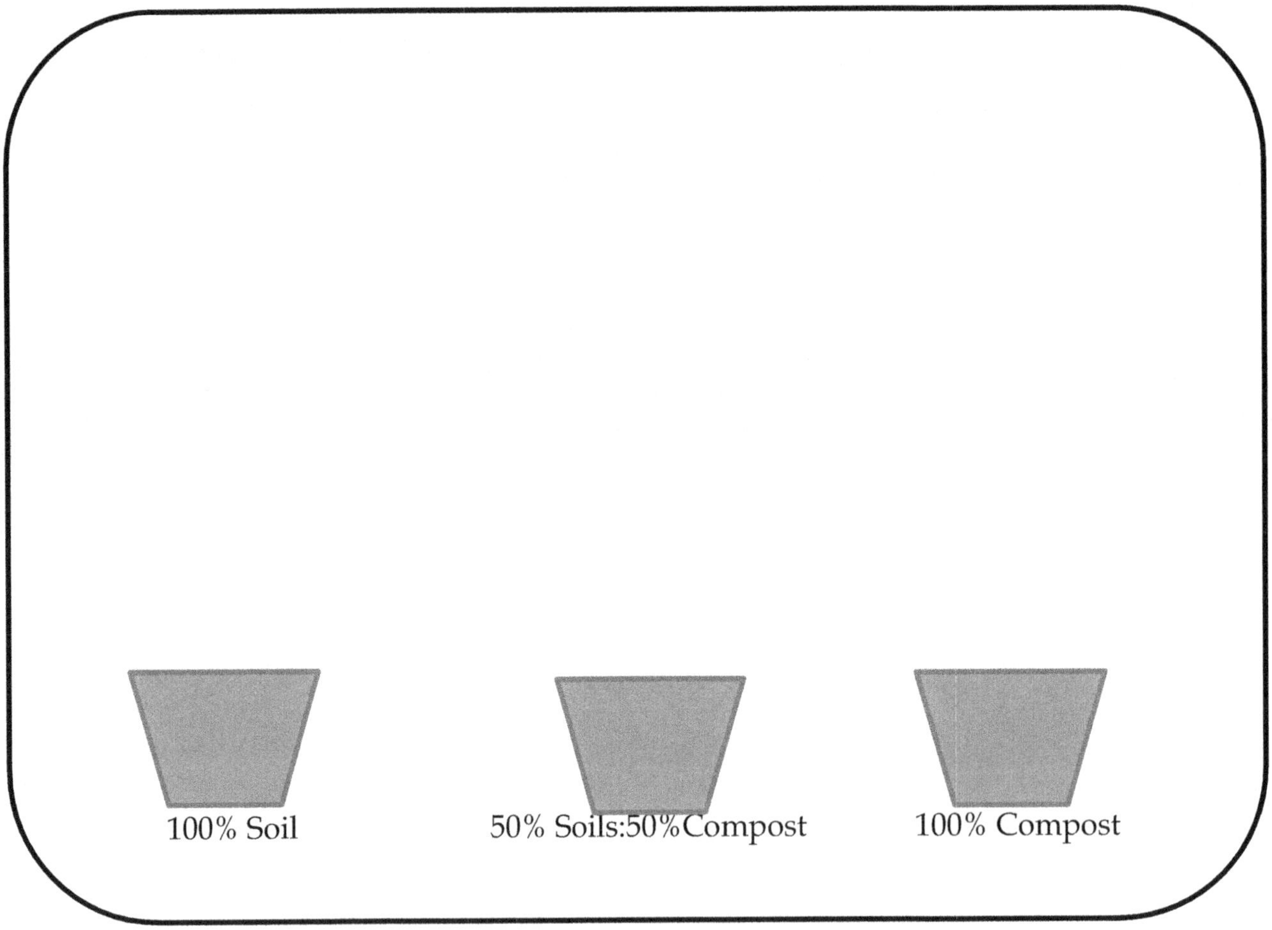

1) In which soil medium did the seeds germinate first?

   100% Soil   50% Soils:50%Compost   100% Compost

2) In which soil medium did you measure the highest growth of stems after a week?

   100% Soil   50% Soils:50%Compost   100% Compost

3) In which soil medium did you count the most numbers of leaves after a week?

   100% Soil   50% Soils:50%Compost   100% Compost

4) Which soil medium did you observe the best growth of plant in general?

   100% Soil   50% Soils:50%Compost   100% Compost

5) Did your hypothesis agree with your results?

   Yes   No

Activity B: Break the Code

A	B	C	D	E	F	G	H	I	J	K	L
!	@	#	$	%	^	&	*	+	~	:	;

M	N	O	P	Q	R	S	T	U	V	W	X	Y	Z
"	<	>	?	/	1	2	3	4	5	6	7	8	9

The three great ways to eliminate waste is to ____ ____ ____ ____ ____,

1 % 4 2 %

____ ____ ____ ____ ____ ____, and ____ ____ ____ ____ ____ ____ ____.

1 % $ 4 # % 1 % # 8 # ; %

One way to reduce waste is by ____ ____ ____ ____ ____ ____ ____ ____ ____ ____.

> " ? > 2 3 + < &

____ ____ ____ ____ ____ ____ ____ ____ ____ ____ ____ are organisms that break down dead or decaying

$ % # > " ? > 2 % 1 2

organisms. They use ____ ____ ____ ____ ____ ____ ____

> 1 & ! < + #

____ ____ ____ ____ ____ ____ ____ ____ ____ as sources of energy or food.

" ! 3 % 1 + ! ; 2

____ ____ ____ ____ ____ ____ ____ is the end product of decomposition.

> " ? > 2 3

Unit 17: The Water Cycle & Soil

- ☐ LESSON A: Observation and Discussion
  - Read the lesson carefully to make sure you have all needed supplies and you understand the content.
  - Observation Record: Draw what you observe inside the bag for five days. Note any changes you see.
- ☐ ACTIVITY A: Focus on Vocabulary
  - Draw the symbol of the different parts of the water cycle and label the diagram using the given definition.
- ☐ ACTIVITY B: Fun Facts
  - Matching type. Trace the lines to match the statement on the left with the water facts on the right.
- ☐ ACTIVITY C: Nature Journaling
  - Have your student draw the location where you went on a nature walk and any sign of parts of the water cycle that you observed. Identify in your picture what part/s of the water cycle you observed and write a paragraph about it
- ☐ PARENT NOTES:

____

____

____

____

____

Lesson A: The Water Cycle of Soil in a Baggy

Objectives:

1. To learn about different uses of water.
2. To model water cycle in a closed system model.
3. To discuss the importance of conserving water.

Before the Lesson:

- Conduct science outside, whenever possible—check the lesson type and the weather.
- Gather and prep all materials.

Materials Needed:

- ☐ 2-3 Plants grown from Unit 16 or any seedlings
- ☐ Water bottle
- ☐ Scissors
- ☐ Small rocks
- ☐ Potting soil
- ☐ 1 gallon Ziplock bag
- ☐ Observation Record "Water Cycle in a Baggie"

In Class:

7. Class Observation:
   - ☐ Review what you have learned about soil and composting.
   - ☐ Ask what did they have to do to make sure their plants grow last week.

     The student has to water their seeds to germinate and grow. You can review how plants absorbed water through the roots and how it travels from the roots to the stems and leaves.
   - ☐ Ask the student what happened to the water that has been absorbed by plants.

     Most of the water, about 95%, that the plant absorbed is transpired back to the atmosphere. The rate of transpiration depends on the temperature, humidity soil moisture and types of plants.

- Transpiration is the process by which water is carried from the roots, to the small pores on the underside of plant leaves where water evaporates and released back to the atmosphere.

8. Class Activity:

   . Tell the students that they will model water cycle using some of the plants they grew from last week.

   a. Cut a water bottle in half. You will only need the bottom half.
   b. Place small rocks at the bottom of the water bottle for drainage. Get some plants from the planter you used from Unit 16 and placed them on top of the small rocks.
   c. Fill the container with potting soil.
   d. Water your plants.
   e. Placed the potted plants inside the 1 gallon Ziplock bag and seal.
   f. Placed the sealed bag with plants next to a window sill or any place in the house that gets sunlight.
   g. Observe your plants and bag every day. Record your observations every day for five days on your Observation Record "Water Cycle in a Baggie".

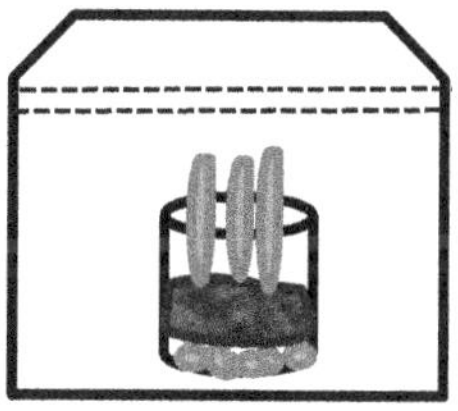

9. Class processing:

   . Ask the students why water is important to us and our planet?

   a. Can they name different places they can find water in nature/water reservoir?

      Oceans, lakes, ponds, rivers, glaciers, permafrost, ground water.

      In what form water exist in the natural world?

      As snow, rain, clouds.

   - Tell the students that the amount of water on Earth is fairly constant and that water moves from different water reservoir mentioned above through the process of water cycle. Their experiment this week will show them how water can change phases as it moves from one reservoir to the next.

Observation Record

Day 1

Note: ____

Day 2

Note: ____

Day 3

Note: ______________________________

Day 4

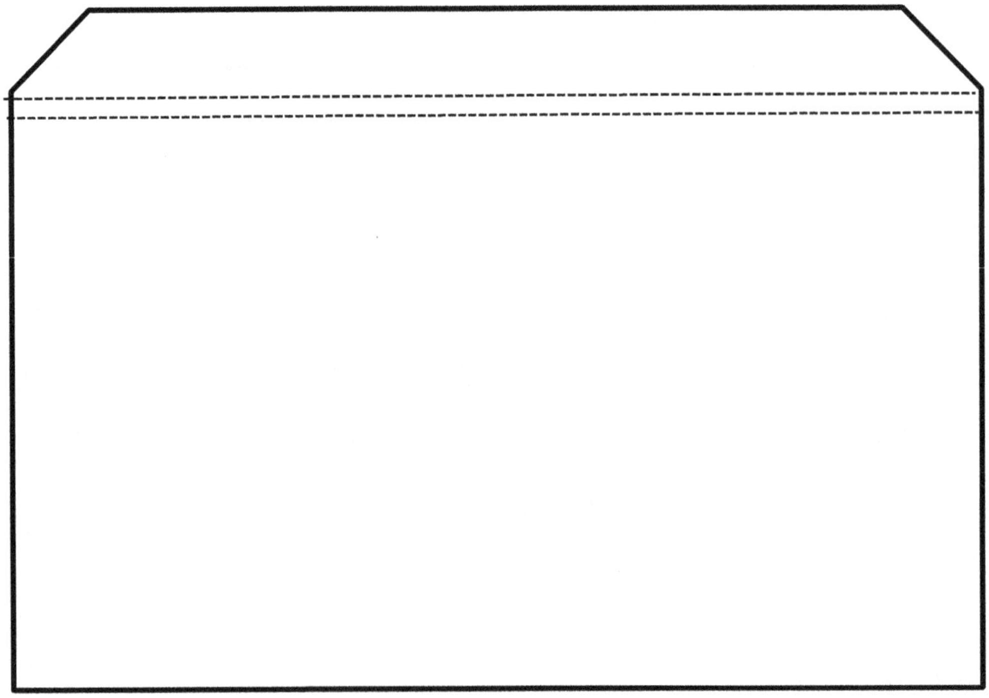

Note: ______________________________

Day 5

Note: ____

Activity A: Water Cycle

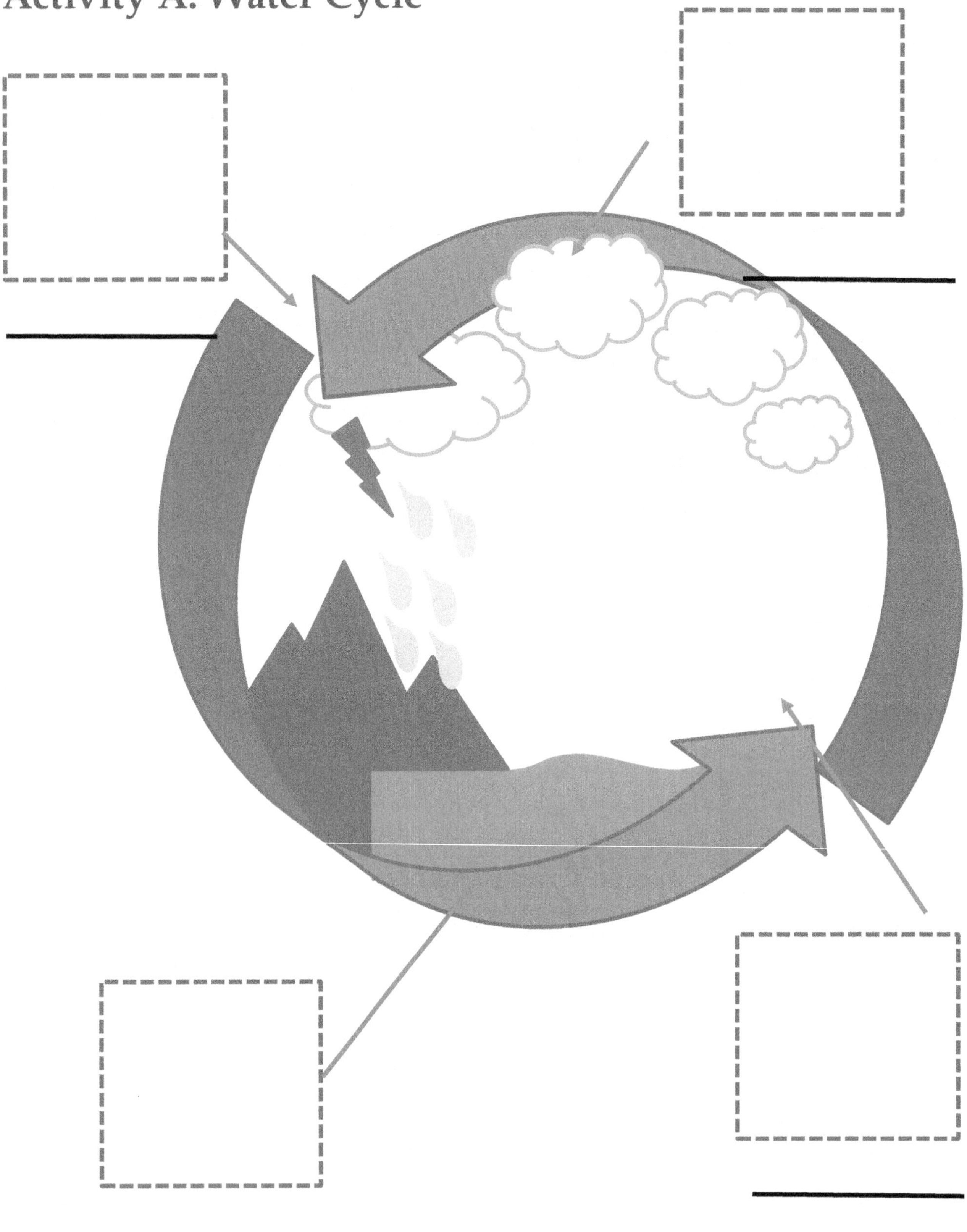

EVAPORATION: Movement of water as water vapor to air from different water reservoir such as oceans, pond and lakes, and ground.

CONDENSATION- The transformation of water vapor in the atmosphere into liquid water droplets as clouds or fog.

PRECIPITATION – Condensed water droplets that fall to the Earth's surface mostly as rain but can also be in the form of sleet, snow, or hail.

RUN-OFF – The movement of water across the land which can include surface run-off, seepage underground, or storage in bodies of water.

Activity B: Facts about Water

These elements made up water molecule.

Water covers this much of the Earth's surface.

Water freezes at this temperature and boils at this temperature.

Water has three phases, _______ as ice, _____ as water, and ______ as water vapor.

The longest river system in the United States is the ___

0°C
100°C

Solid, Liquid and Gas

Hydrogen and Oxygen

Mississippi and Missouri River

About 70%

Activity C: My Nature Walk & Signs of the Water Cycle

Date: ____________________

Unit 18: Weather and Climate

- ☐ LESSON A: Observation and Discussion
  - o Read the lesson carefully to make sure you have all needed supplies and you understand the content.
  - o Observation Record: Starting from the bottom, color each circle base on the color of the candy that you drew from the bag representing the daily weather condition.
- ☐ ACTIVITY A: Nature Journaling
  - o Collect temperature data either using internet information or recording from actual observation using window thermometer.
  - o When collecting the data, make sure that you are recording the temperature at the same time each day. Record other weather parameters using the Weather Data Sheet provided below.
  - o Summarize your data at the end of the week.
- ☐ ACTIVITY B: Focus on Vocabulary
  - o Write "W' on the space if the description pertains to weather condition and write "C" on the space provided if the description pertains to climate.
- ☐ ACTIVITY C: Focus on Vocabulary
  - o Color the map to show the different climate zone in North America. Assign different colors for different climate zones using the legend to the right of the map.
- ☐ PARENT NOTES:

Lesson A: Weather and Climate

Objectives:

1. To have an understanding of the difference between weather and climate.
2. To determine and record weather conditions in a given set of time.

Before the Lesson:

Conduct science outside, whenever possible—check the lesson type and the weather.

Gather and prep all materials.

Materials Needed:

- A small bag of candy that has different colors (at least 5 different color in a bag)
- Observation Record "Weather in a Candy Bag"

In Class:

1. Class Observation:
   - Ask students to look outside. What is the weather doing right now?

     Is it sunny or cloudy? How much clouds are there? Ask the students if they can gather all the clouds that they can see, would it fill a whole circle? Half of a circle? A quarter of a circle?
   - Remind the students about what they learned about the water cycle. Is there any precipitation? If yes, what kind? Is it raining? snowing? Are there any thunderstorms?
   - Ask the students if the weather today is the same as yesterday or the day before?
   - Can they predict the weather for tomorrow? Ask the students to explain their answer.
   - Ask students to think of what the condition like during the different seasons where you live.

     Ask students to fill in the following sentences. During the wintertime it is usually (hot or cold) outside. During the summer time it is usually (hot or cold) outside. What about in the Spring or Fall? Which season rains a lot?
2. Class Activity:

a. Tell the students that they will pretend to be meteorologist.

Meteorologist is a scientist that study the atmospheric condition to predict and forecast weather.

b. Ask the students different weather condition that they can think of and assign a weather condition to a color of a candy. Example yellow candy means Sunny, blue is for rainy, green for cloudy and so on. The number of weather conditions depend on the number of different colors found inside the candy bag. You can also assign the weather condition to a particular color ahead of time.

c. Make a small tear at one end of the bag and ask the student that they can only get one candy at a time. Using the tally sheet provided as Observation Record "Weather in a Candy Bag", color the circle for each weather condition that correspond to the color of the candy that comes out. Continue with this step until all the candies have been taken out (or stop at 30 candies to represent the days in a month.)

3. Class processing:

a. Tell the students that each time they draw one candy from the bag, it represents the weather condition for that day.

b. Tally the number of candies for each color/weather condition. Which candy color has the most number? If each candy represents the weather for a particular day, what does the most number color candy represent for a longer period of time? You can discuss that by looking at several weather data for a period of time, meteorologist can look for trends which they can use to describe the climate in a given area for a period of time. One can also describe climate as the avergae weather in a given area. Just like in our model using candies in a bag, the most color candy can tell us that for that 30 day period/month, we can say that the average weather or climate is sunny, or rainy depending on which color candy has the most in number.

4. Class Discussion:

- Is it usually hot where you live?
- Is it usually cold where you live?
- Does it rain often where you live?
- What is the weather today?
- What is the climate during the winter month? Summer months?

Observation Record: Weather in a Candy Bag

TOTAL=							
○	○	○	○	○	○	○	○
○	○	○	○	○	○	○	○
○	○	○	○	○	○	○	○
○	○	○	○	○	○	○	○
○	○	○	○	○	○	○	○
○	○	○	○	○	○	○	○
○	○	○	○	○	○	○	○
○	○	○	○	○	○	○	○
○	○	○	○	○	○	○	○
○	○	○	○	○	○	○	○
SUNNY	PARTIALLY SUNNY	CLOUDY	RAIN CLOUDS WITH THUNDER STORMS	RAINSHOWERS	RAINY		

1) Tally the total number of circles that you shaded for each color candy/daily weather condition. Place your total on the topmost box.
2) Which color candy has the most number?

    ____

3) What weather condition it represents?

    ____

4) If you are going to summarize your data, how would you describe the atmospheric condition for this time period that you sampled?

    For the ________ days we sampled, the condition was mostly

    ____________________.

5) Circle the correct word to complete the sentence.

    Individual color candy represents (WEATHER or CLIMATE) condition for each day.

    The most number color candy represents the (WEATHER or CLIMATE) based on the prevailing conditions for a long period of time.

Activity A: Weather Collection Data

Location:

Date: Time:	Date: Time:
Day 1	Day 2
Temperature: ________ °F	Temperature: ________ °F
Other weather parameters:	Other weather parameters:
Cloudiness (check one)	Cloudiness (check one)
☐ Clear sky with no clouds	☐ Clear sky with no clouds
☐ Clear sky with some clouds	☐ Clear sky with some clouds
☐ Most of the sky is covered with clouds	☐ Most of the sky is covered with clouds
☐ No sky showing, all clouds	☐ No sky showing, all clouds
Precipitation (check one)	Precipitation (check one)
☐ Shower	☐ Shower
☐ Heavy rain	☐ Heavy rain
☐ Light Snow falling	☐ Light Snow falling
☐ Heavy Snow falling	☐ Heavy Snow falling
☐ Hails	☐ Hails
☐ Others ________________	☐ Others ________________
Wind (Check one)	Wind (Check one)
☐ No wind	☐ No wind
☐ Light wind	☐ Light wind
☐ Strong wind	☐ Strong wind

Date: Time:	Date: Time:
Day 3	Day 4
Temperature: _________ °F	Temperature: _________ °F
Other weather parameters:	Other weather parameters:
Cloudiness (check one)	Cloudiness (check one)
☐ Clear sky with no clouds	☐ Clear sky with no clouds
☐ Clear sky with some clouds	☐ Clear sky with some clouds
☐ Most of the sky is covered with clouds	☐ Most of the sky is covered with clouds
☐ No sky showing, all clouds	☐ No sky showing, all clouds
Precipitation (check one)	Precipitation (check one)
☐ Shower	☐ Shower
☐ Heavy rain	☐ Heavy rain
☐ Light Snow falling	☐ Light Snow falling
☐ Heavy Snow falling	☐ Heavy Snow falling
☐ Hails	☐ Hails
☐ Others _________________	☐ Others _________________
Wind (Check one)	Wind (Check one)
☐ No wind	☐ No wind
☐ Light wind	☐ Light wind
☐ Strong wind	☐ Strong wind
Draw your observation:	Draw your observation:
Date: Time:	Date: Time:

Day 5	Day 6
Temperature: ________ °F	Temperature: ________ °F
Other weather parameters:	Other weather parameters:
Cloudiness (check one)	Cloudiness (check one)
☐ Clear sky with no clouds	☐ Clear sky with no clouds
☐ Clear sky with some clouds	☐ Clear sky with some clouds
☐ Most of the sky is covered with clouds	☐ Most of the sky is covered with clouds
☐ No sky showing, all clouds	☐ No sky showing, all clouds
Precipitation (check one)	Precipitation (check one)
☐ Shower	☐ Shower
☐ Heavy rain	☐ Heavy rain
☐ Light Snow falling	☐ Light Snow falling
☐ Heavy Snow falling	☐ Heavy Snow falling
☐ Hails	☐ Hails
☐ Others ________________	☐ Others ________________
Wind (Check one)	Wind (Check one)
☐ No wind	☐ No wind
☐ Light wind	☐ Light wind
☐ Strong wind	☐ Strong wind
Draw your observation:	Draw your observation:

Activity B: Weather vs. Climate

________ I look outside and the rain is pouring so I decided to wear my raincoat and boots before going outside.

________ It is hot and humid in the summer months.

________ I heard the news person while watching TV that today is going to be sunny but the highest temperature would only be 30°F.

________ It snowed last night and the total accumulation is 6 inches.

________ In our area, the lowest average temperature always recorded is in February.

________ In tropical places, the rainy season is also called the monsoon when most of a region's average annual rainfall occurs.

________ My umbrella flipped over as I am walking from school this afternoon due to strong winds.

________ The average annual rainfall in very dry places is usually below 10 inches.

________ I got sunburned from playing outside yesterday.

________ I have to wear my coat, hat and gloves today because it is very cold.

Activity C: Mapping Climate Zones

North America Climate Zones

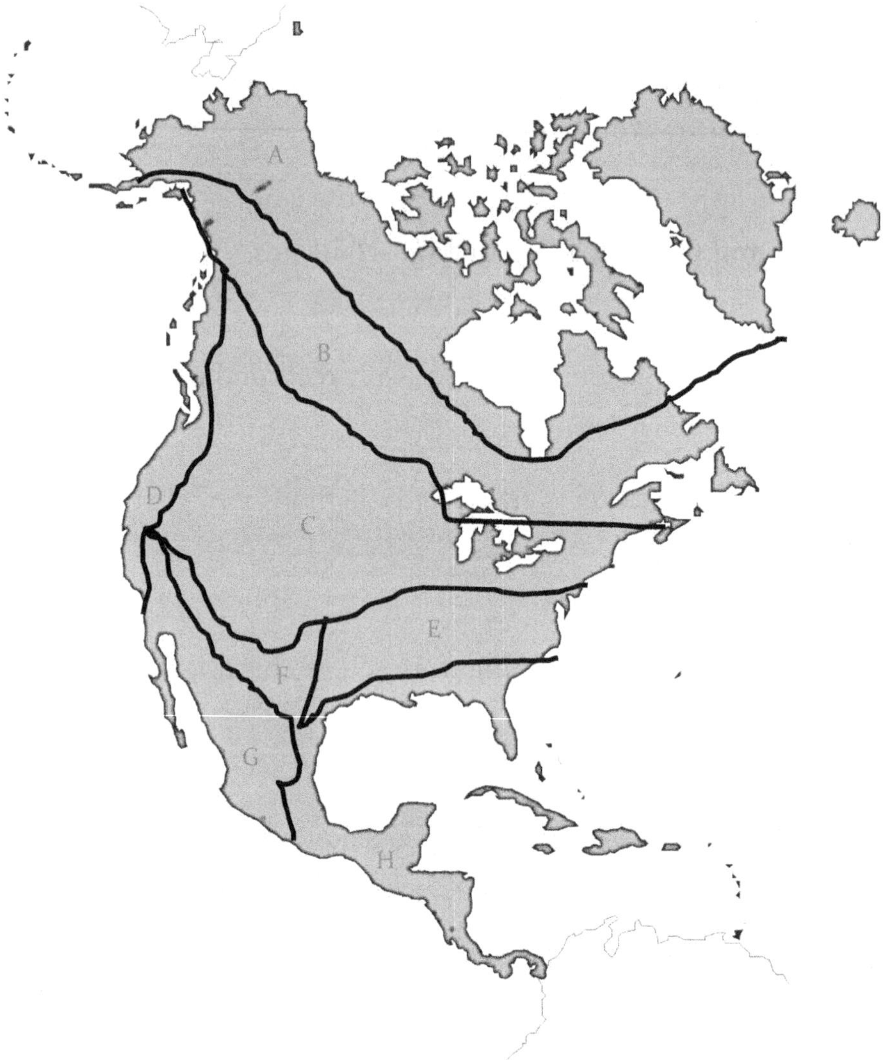

LEGEND:

A) Subarctic/Arctic

B) Very Cold

C) Cold

D) Marine

E) Mixed Humid

F) Mixed Dry

G) Hot dry

H) Hot Humid

Unit 19: Ocean Zones

- ☐ LESSON A: Observation and Discussion
  - Read the lesson carefully to make sure you have all needed supplies and you understand the content.
- ☐ ACTIVITY A: Experiment
  - The purpose of this activity is to review concepts learned from Lesson A about the different ocean zones. By doing the ocean zones in the bottle, students can visualize the different depths of each layers and how much light can penetrate through the layers.
  - Ocean Zones Record Sheet: Use colored pencils to color the bottle to match what your bottle looks like. Make notes about what type of plants or animals might live in each layer (zone).
- ☐ ACTIVITY B: Research
  - Pick a marine organism and fill up the information about that organisms. Parents can help students to get library books or research on-line to fill up the following information.
- ☐ ACTIVITY C: Focus on Vocabulary
  - Fold along the solid lines and cut along the dash lines. Look at the definition side and identify what is being defined. You can challenge yourself by looking at the term and try to define the term. Play alone or quiz each other. Laminate the cards if needed.
- ☐ PARENT NOTES:

Lesson A: Ocean Zones Scroll

Objectives:

1. To introduce students to the different ocean zones.
2. To be familiar with plants and animals that live at different ocean zones.

Before the Lesson:

2. Conduct science outside, whenever possible—check the lesson type and the weather.

3. Gather and prep all materials.

Materials Needed:

- ☐ Paper towel tube
- ☐ Yarn or string
- ☐ Coloring utensils (crayons or colored pencils)
- ☐ Scissors
- ☐ Glue
- ☐ Construction paper one of each color (light blue, dark blue and black)

In Class:

1. Class Observation:
   - ☐ Ask students if they have ever been to the ocean.
   - ☐ What can they tell about the ocean?

   This will be a good time to review landforms and bodies of water that was discussed in Unit 11.

   - ☐ Has anyone been swimming in the ocean?
   - ☐ Has anyone been sailing on the ocean?
   - ☐ Has anyone gone snorkeling?
   - ☐ Can they guess how deep is the ocean?

   The average depth of the ocean is about 4,000 meters which is actually half the height of the tallest mountain in the world which is Mount Everest that is around 8,800 meter high above sea level.

- Ask students if they know anything about the different depths of the ocean, such as what animals can be found there. Could a whale swim near the shore, for instance?

2. Class Activity:

   a. Tell the students that they will be learning about the different layers or zones of the ocean from the surface to the seafloor.

   b. Below is a table summarizing the different parameters associated with the different ocean zones (source: oceanexplorer.noaa.gov). You can read the description and the students can write the facts about the zones and draw different creatures that can be found in each zone.

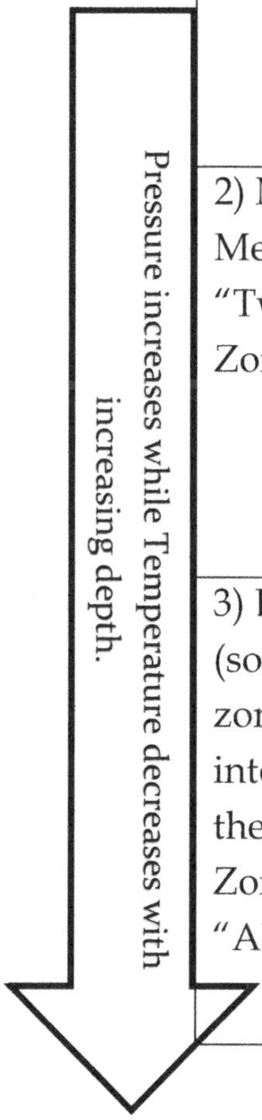
Pressure increases while Temperature decreases with increasing depth.

ZONES	DEPTH	LIGHT	ORGANISMS
1) Epipelagic or "Photic Zone"	0-200 m	Sunlight penetrates sufficiently to support growth of microalgae and macroalgae. 90% of marine animals are found here.	Phytoplankton, zooplankton, seaweeds, jelly fish, sharks, dolphins, sea turtles, seals, sea lions, sting rays, mackerel, tuna.
2) Midwater/ Mesopelagic or "Twilight Zone"	200-1,000 m	Light penetration is very minimal since light decreases greatly with increasing depth. No plants grow in this zone.	Squid, cuttlefish, larger fish swordfish that migrates to the epipelagic zone at night time to feed.
3) Bathypelagic (sometimes this zone is divided into two parts; the "Apothic Zone" and the "Abyss"	1,000-Sea Floor	No sunlight penetrates this depth. This zone is in total darkness. Pressure is really high and water temperature is near freezing.	Giant squid, bioluminescent organisms, angler fish, hatchet fish, tubeworms, seaspiders.

3. Class processing:
    - What would be some adaptations of animals living at various ocean zones that can help them survive better in that environment?
4. Class Discussion:
    - What did you learn from this activity?
    - How does it help you to understand the ocean zones better?

Activity A: Ocean Zone in a Bottle

Materials Needed:

- ☐ (1) Pencil per student
- ☐ (1) Set of colored pencils per student
- ☐ (1) Observation Record "Ocean Zones in a Bottle"
- ☐ (1) Empty water bottle with cap per student
- ☐ (1/3 cup) Small dark rocks, black fish tank rocks, or sand per student
- ☐ (2/3 cup) Corn syrup
- ☐ (2/3 cup) Blue dish soap per student
- ☐ (2/3 cup) Cooking Oil per student
- ☐ (1/3 cup) 91% alcohol
- ☐ (1) Dropper/pipette or syringe
- ☐ (1) Set of food coloring (black or purple, green has to be oil based and blue) per classroom
- ☐ (1) Funnel (or small paper to use as a funnel) per student
- ☐ (1) Flashlight per student
- ☐ (1) Smock per student
- ☐ (1) Plastic fork per student
- ☐ (5) Small cups to put the ingredients into per student
- ☐ (1) Bottle of cleaning spray per classroom
- ☐ Tape

Class Activity:

- ☐ Introduce the activity "Ocean Zones in a Bottle" by telling the students they will be creating their own mini-ocean layers inside a bottle.
- ☐ Put on smocks.
- ☐ Hand out materials needed for the Ocean Zones in a Bottle activity.
- ☐ Work together to carefully to add each layer to the bottle using the funnel.

□ First, create the bottom layer, by adding dark colored rocks or sand to represent the seafloor.

□ Next, add black or purple food coloring to the corn syrup and mix it with the fork. This should create a very dark colored liquid. You can use a dark corn syrup.

- □ Pour the darkly colored corn syrup on top of the rocks. This represents the abyssal zone.
- □ Now add the blue colored dish soap on top of the corn syrup. This represents the midnight or aphotic zone. Both the abyssal and midnight zone are sometimes called as the Bathypelagic zone together.
- □ Take the cooking oil, add a drop of green food coloring to the oil cup. Use a plastic fork to mix the food coloring and oil together. You have to use an oil-based food coloring so that the food color and oil would mix. Add food coloring if needed. This represents the Mesopelagic (Twilight) Zone.
- □ Lastly, add one drop of yellow food coloring to the alcohol and using a dropper, carefully pour the alcohol on the side of the bottle to avoid mixing with the other layers. This represents the Epipelagic (Sunlight) Zone. *N.B. Do not shake the bottle as layers will separate.
- □ Use flashlight to light up the back side of the bottle to see the layers better.
- □ Use colored pencils to record findings on the Ocean Zones Record Sheet.
- □ Encourage the students to draw different organism that are found in each layer.
- □ Cut and match the name of the ocean layer and facts about that layer to the layers you created in the bottle. You can tape the cut out on the bottle to label the different layers.

Ocean Zones Record Sheet

Epipelagic (Sunlight)

Mesopelagic (Twilight)

Bathypelagic

Apothic (Midnight)

Abyssal (Abyss)

Seafloor

Epipelagic (Sunlight)- Sunlight penetrates sufficiently to support growth of microalgae and macroalgae. 90% of marine animals are found here.
Depth: 0-200m.

Mesopelagic (Twilight)- Light penetration is very minimal since light decreases greatly with increasing depth. No plants grow in this zone.
Depth: 200-1,000m

Bathypelagic
(Apothic and Abyssal Zone) -
No sunlight penetrates this depth. This zone is in total darkness. Pressure is really high and water temperature is near freezing.
Depth: 1,00m to the seafloor

Activity B: Marine Organisms Research

Facts About My Marine Organism

Name:

____

Draw a picture or cut and paste a picture of the marine organism.

Food I love to eat!

I am located at the ______________________ zone of the ocean.

In order for me to be avoid being eaten by my predators, that help my survival skills, I have these following adaptations:

____

____

____

______________________________.

Activity C: Ocean Facts Card Game

EPIPELAGIC ZONE	This ocean zone is also called the "Photic" zone because sunlight penetrates sufficiently to

MESOPELAGIC ZONE	This zone has very minimal light that can penetrate through it thus it is sometimes called the "Twilight" zone.

BATHYPELAGIC ZONE	No sunlight penetrates this depth. This zone is in total darkness.

PHYTOPLANKTON	These microscopic organisms are the primary producers in the marine environment and are found in the photic zone.

2-3%	Only a small portion of the ocean that light can penetrate. What percent of the ocean is covered by the Epipelagic Zone?

90%	The largest portion of the ocean is devoid of light. What percent of the ocean is covered by the Bathypelagic Zone?

COUNTERSHADING	Some fish in the mesopelagic zone use this strategy where the coloration of their bottom part is lighter while the top part is darker. It is a form or camouflage.

VERTICAL MIGRATION	Due to small amount of food present in the mesopelagic zone, some organisms move to the epipelagic zone at night time to feed. This behavior is commonly called as _____.

PHOTOPHORES	These light-emitting organs found in fish and invertebrates such as squid produce light that match the intensity of light coming from above to conceal the organism from predators.
OCEAN TRENCH	The deepest part of the ocean and can have a depth between 7,000-11,000 meter.

Unit 20: The Atmosphere's Layers

- ☐ LESSON A: Observation and Discussion
  - Read the lesson carefully to make sure you have all needed supplies and you understand the content.
  - Observation Record: The Atmosphere's Layers
- ☐ ACTIVITY A: Experiment
  - The purpose of this activity is to apply your knowledge about what you learn about air pressure and weather by making a weather instrument that measures air pressure to predict weather.
- ☐ ACTIVITY B: Research
  - Label the map of the United States using (cut and paste) the symbol provided, and the weather forecast that is presented by Mr. Weatherman below. Answer the following questions about the weather map you made.
- ☐ ACTIVITY C: Nature Journaling
  - Lay on the ground and draw what you see in the sky. Dictate or write what you observe.
- ☐ PARENT NOTES:

____

____

____

____

Lesson A: Atmosphere's Layers

Objectives:

1. To introduce students to the different layers of the atmosphere.
2. To be familiar with different natural and man-made objects that can be located at different layers of the atmosphere.
3. To create a 2D model of the layers of the atmosphere

Before the Lesson:

2. Conduct science outside, whenever possible—check the lesson type and the weather.

3. Gather and prep all materials.

Materials Needed:

- ☐ Different construction paper (brown, white, yellow, light blue, dark blue, and gray)
- ☐ Writing materials
- ☐ Coloring utensils (crayons or colored pencils)
- ☐ Scissors
- ☐ Glue

In Class:

1. Class Observation:
   - ☐ Ask students what they think about the sky.
   - ☐ Do they look at it each day?
   - ☐ Do they consider how large it is? How far it goes away from us?
   - ☐ Do they consider what it is made of?
   - ☐ Do they take time to watch the clouds float by?
   - ☐ Do they take time to watch the starts at night?
   - ☐ Do they contemplate the different colors of the sunrise and the sunset?
2. Class Activity:

a. Tell the students that they will be learning about the different layers of the atmosphere and categorize them based on temperature, pressure and different natural and man-made objects that can be observed at various layers.

b. Below is a table summarizing the different layers of the atmosphere and some of their characteristics. Source: https://www.nasa.gov

LAYERS OF THE ATMOSPHERE	*THICKNESS*	*TEMPERATURE*	*SOME FACTS*
EXOSPHERE	6,200 miles (up to 10,000 km)	The temperature in the exosphere varies from 0°C to 1700°C because this layer is almost a vacuum (very thin air).	-The upper limit of the Earth's atmosphere. -Air is extremely thin in this layer.
THERMOSPHERE	372 miles (600 km)	The hottest layer of the Earth's atmosphere.	-Auroras (northern and southern lights) occur in this layer. -Satellites are found in the thermosphere. -Absence of water vapor.
MESOSPHERE	53 miles (85 km)	This is the coolest part of the Earth's atmosphere.	-Meteors burn up in this layer. -This layer can only be access by used of rockets.
STRATOSPHERE	31 miles (50 m)	With an increase in altitude, temperature increases due to the absorption of UV rays by the ozone layer.	-The ozone layer is found in stratosphere. The ozone helps absorbs and scatter UV rays from the sun. -The highest height that an aircraft can reach.
TROPHOSPHERE	5-9 miles (8-14.5 km)	With an increase in elevation, there is a decrease in temperature.	-The densest part of the atmosphere. 75% of the Earth's mass is in the troposphere. -Most of the weather happens in this layer since most of the water vapor is present in this layer.
Earth			

Pressure decreases with increasing height from the Earth's Surface

- Fold the gray construction paper in half cross-wise and make a half-circle shape from it (dimension of 9in width and 6in height).
- Do the same thing for the other colors having the following dimensions (width x height): Dark blue (8x4.5 in), Light blue (7x4 in), Yellow (6x3.5 in), White (5x3 in), Brown (4x2.5 in)

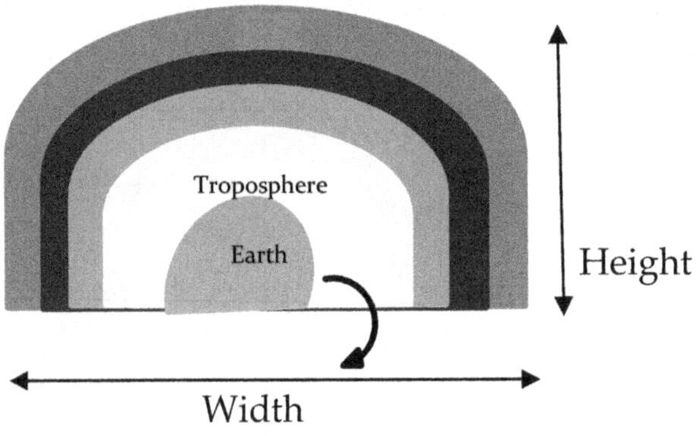

- You can pre-cut the shapes and the students can staple them together.
- Staple the bottom part together.
- Write the names of the different layers of the atmosphere on the exposed portion of the construction paper. Label the brown construction paper as the Earth, the white construction paper as the troposphere (as shown in the above image) and so on. This will look like a mini-booklet.
- Starting from the troposphere, read and discuss the different characteristics of each layer and some important facts about that layer using the table above or you can also use other reference text book for additional information. Flip the page and write on the exposed page. For older students that can write independently, ask the students to write the information they heard for each layer on as you discuss them.
- For younger students, you can use the information available in Observation Record "Atmosphere's Layers" by cutting and pasting them in their booklet.
- Ask students to draw objects that are found in each layer and color their picture.

3. Class processing:
    - Ask the students why astronauts need to wear space suit when they work outside the space station in space? Mention that it has something to do with temperature, pressure and air.
    - What happen to the air pressure as we ascend from Earth?

The air pressure becomes less. On the other hand, air pressure increases as we go underwater.

Imagine a marshmallow being sent to outer space without a space suit, what do you think will happen to the size of the marshmallow? *It will expand and eventually pop.*

4. Class Discussion:

 - What did you learn from this activity?
 - How does it help you to understand the layers of the atmosphere?

Observation Record: The Atmosphere's Layers

EXOSPHERE

Thickness of 6,200 miles (up to 10,000 km)	The temperature in the exosphere varies from 0°C to 1700°C because this layer is almost a vacuum (very thin air).	-The upper limit of the Earth's atmosphere. -Air is extremely thin in this layer.

THERMOSPHERE

372 miles (600 km)	The hottest layer of the Earth's atmosphere.	-Auroras (northern and southern lights) occur in this layer. -Satellites are found in the thermosphere. -Absence of water vapor.

MESOSPHERE

53 miles (85 km)	This is the coolest part of the Earth's atmosphere.	-Meteors burn up in this layer. -This layer can only be access by used of rockets.

STRATOSPHERE

31 miles (50 km)	With an increase in altitude, temperature increases due to the absorption of UV rays by the ozone layer.	-The ozone layer is found in stratosphere. The ozone helps absorbs and scatter UV rays from the sun. -The highest height that an aircraft can reach.

TROPHOSPHERE

5-9 miles (8-14.5 km)	With an increase in elevation, there is a decrease in temperature.	-The densest part of the atmosphere. 75% of the Earth's mass is in the troposphere. -Most of the weather happens in this layer since most of the water vapor is present in this layer.

Activity A: Measuring Air Pressure Using a Barometer

Materials Needed:

- ☐ Wide mouth glass jar
- ☐ Balloon
- ☐ Rubber band
- ☐ Plastic straw
- ☐ scissors
- ☐ A piece of double-sided tape
- ☐ A piece of white paper

Class Activity:

- ☐ Cut the opening of the balloon so that it can fit over the mouth of the glass jar.
- ☐ Secure the balloon using rubber band.
- ☐ Cut one end of the plastic straw so that it becomes pointy. 
- ☐ Place the double-sided tape at the center of the balloon and attach the straw on it having the pointy end hanging out.
- ☐ Make sure that the straw is level.

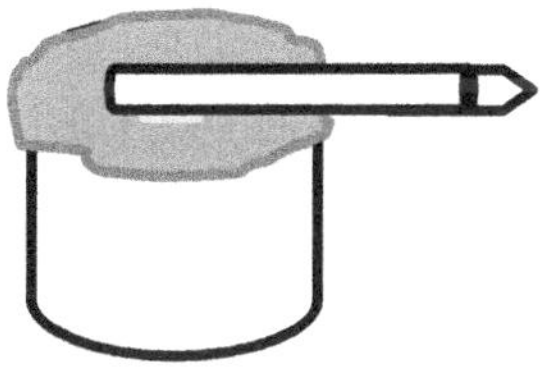

- ☐ Place your DIY barometer on a flat stable surface, preferably next to a wall, away from direct sunlight.
- ☐ Tape the white paper on the wall and mark on the paper where the point of the straw rest.

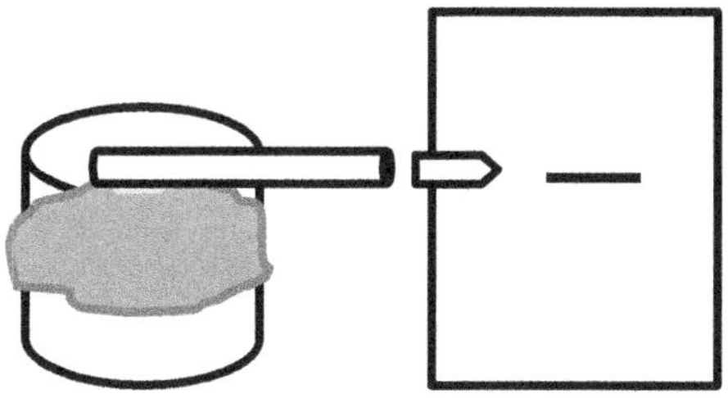

This will be your reference point. At this time,

the pressure inside the glass jar is equal to the

surrounding air pressure outside the jar, hence

the balloon is leveled.

- When the ambient or surrounding pressure drops or becomes lower than the inside of the jar, the balloon will be pushed up making the straw tilt downward below the reference line. This indicates humid or rainy days are coming.

- When the ambient or surrounding pressure increases or becomes higher than the inside of the jar, the balloon will be pushed down making the straw tilt upward below the reference line. This indicates dry and cool weather is coming.

- If the straw hasn't changed its position, it means that there will be no drastic change in the weather pattern for the next day.
- Record your observation and predictions below. Try to see if the prediction the you made the day before based on the barometer reading correspond to the current weather.

Barometer Reading (*Above, Level* or *Below*)	Weather prediction (*Dry/cool* OR *Humid/Rainy*)	Actual weather the day after your prediction	Is your prediction *Similar* or *Different* than actual

Activity B: Weather Map

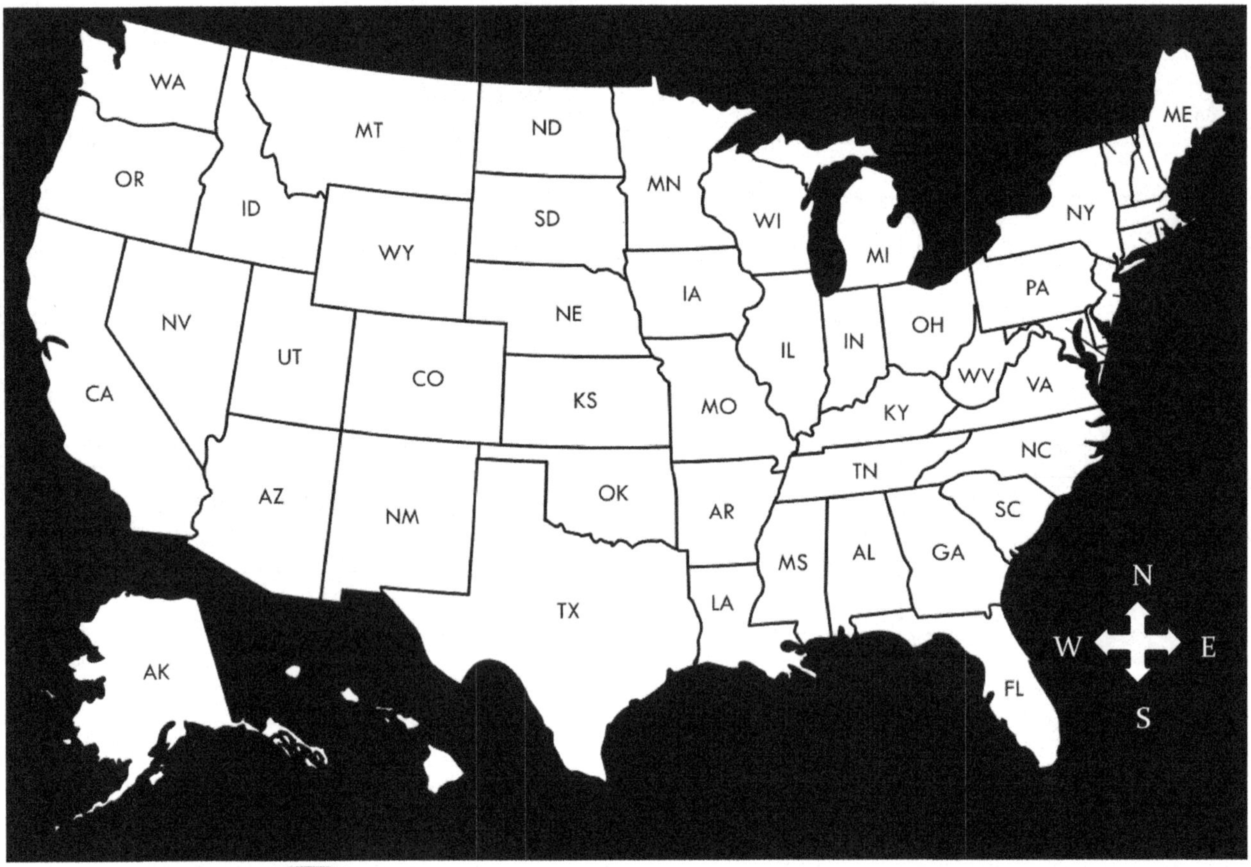

Hello, welcome to our weather forecast for tomorrow!
A low pressure is moving into the **Southwest Region** of the United States so this area will experience scattered rain showers and thunderstorms. **The Northeast Region** will be sunny and warm while the **Southeast** will be cloudy. The **Central United States** will experience moderate winds towards the afternoon.

Cut the symbols below and paste them in the appropriate regions of the United States that were mentioned in the weather forecast.

1) If you live in Arizona (AZ), would you plan to bring an umbrella and wear a raincoat when you leave the house the next day? Why or Why not?

2) What kind of clothing would you wear the next day if you live in Massachusetts (MA) based on the weather forecast?

3) If you live in Georgia (GA) what would you tell your mom if she plans to wash and hang clothes outside the next day?

4) If you live in Kansas (KS), would it be ideal to fly your kite after lunch with your friends?

   Why or Why not?

Activity C: Nature Journaling

Unit 21: The Water Cycle

☐ LESSON A: Observation and Discussion

- Read the lesson carefully to make sure you have all needed supplies and you understand the content.
- Observation Record: Draw the solar sill before placing it under the sun and after a few hours. Using the terms for water cycle, EVAPORATION, CONDENSATION, PRECIPITATION and RESERVOIR, label your picture below. Use arrows to show the flow of water in the cycle.

☐ ACTIVITY A: Focus on Vocabulary

- Cut along broken lines and fold along solid lines. Place the folded side upward (the picture should be showing). Color the picture and label the different parts of the water cycle shown in the diagram. Cut the definitions for each part of the water cycle and glue them inside the corresponding flap.

☐ ACTIVITY B: Focus on Vocabulary

- Follow the instruction to make a water cycle bead bracelet. Each color bead represents a part of a water cycle. This is a fun activity to review the water cycle lesson.

☐ ACTIVITY C: Nature Journaling

- Go on a nature walk and look for a reservoir of water. Discuss what could have been the source of water in that reservoir. Draw your observation and dictate or write possible source/s of water in the reservoir.

☐ PARENT NOTES:

____

____

Lesson A: Water Cycle using Solar Still

Objectives:

1. To provide review and additonal information about the water cycle as a follow-up from the composting unit.

Before the Lesson:

- Conduct science outside, whenever possible—check the lesson type and the weather.
- Gather and prep all materials.

Materials Needed:

- ☐ 1-2 gallon plastic bin or bowl
- ☐ 1-2 L of soil or sand
- ☐ Plastic cup
- ☐ Plastic wrap
- ☐ Tape
- ☐ Small rock
- ☐ 1-2 cups of water
- ☐ 1tbsp of salt
- ☐ Blue food color

In Class:

1. Class Observation:

   ☐ Ask students to recall what they learned about the water cycle in composting.

   ☐ What does water help to do in a compost pile?

   ☐ Does water matter to the farmer?

   ☐ Now, what about rain? Where did it come from and how water ends up in the sky?

   ☐ Does rain matter to the farmer? Does a river, pond, or lake matter to the farmer?

□ What can students tell about the water cycle of rain? Have they observed how this works?

10. Class Activity:

a. Tell the students that they will be observing how water from the ground end up in the atmosphere and eventually in a water reservoir.
b. Place the sand or soil evenly at the bottom of the plastic bin.
c. Secure the plastic cup at the center of the soil or sand by pressing it down.
d. Place 1-2 drops of blue food coloring in 1-2 cups of water. Mix the salt and pour the salty colored water evenly into your soil or sand.
e. Cover the plastic bin with plastic wrap and seal it using tape.
f. Place a small rock on top of the plastic wrap right above the opening of the plastic cup.
g. Tell the students that this set up is called a solar sill.
h. Place the set-up under direct sunlight. Set aside and proceed to Class Processing.
i. It will take 3-4 hours to see water collected inside the plastic cup. You can make another set-up ahead of time in order to show the students what will happen after few hours.

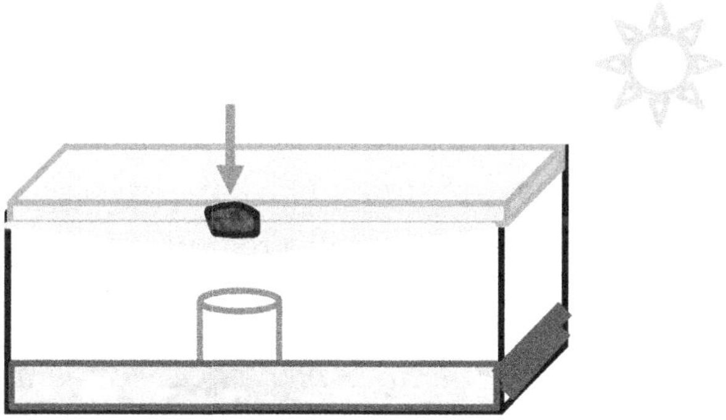

11. Class processing:

□ While the solar sill is heating up under the sun, the students can draw their set-up Observation Record Solar Sill. You can also ask the following questions to the students.

- o Would the water in the soil stay in the soil or will go somewhere else?
- o Where would the water go? What is this process called?
- o Can the water escape from the solar sill? Why? Or Why not?

12. Class Discussion:

- After students give their predictions to what will happen to the water inside the solar sill, observe the solar sill that the class set-up. You might see some water droplets already forming underneath the plastic wrap.
    - Ask the students how did the water ended up there? Remind the students about what they learned in Unit 17. *The energy from the Sun (solar energy) heats up the soil making the water undergo evaporation. Turning liquid water to water vapor or gas.*
    - As the water vapors reached the top and hit the plastic wrap which is cooler because of the cooler air surrounding the outside of the solar sill, they *condense* back to water molecules and become water droplets. You might also see fogging which simulates cloud formation when water droplets started to aggregate or come together.
    - Show the students the solar sill that was set up ahead of time.

      Eventually, the aggregate of water droplets will be too heavy and will start dripping into the plastic cup. This process demonstrates when the clouds become too heavy with water droplets that the water droplets will start to fall back to Earth as *precipitation* (in the form of snow or rain).
    - The plastic cup represents *water reservoir* such as ocean, lakes or ponds where water is stored.

Extension:

- Ask the students what is the color of the water they place in the soil or sand? Is the water collected inside the plastic cup remains blue? You can also ask your student to taste the water collected inside the cup. Is it still salty?

  The water inside the cup is clear and without salt. Why is that? Explain to the students that when water evaporates, only the water molecules change from liquid to gas and any pollutants or impurities like salt are left behind.

  The solar sill is used to distill or purify water using the heat from the sun to evaporate, cool and collect clean water from dirty or impure water source.

- State of matter: You can discuss to students that water can be in three different states of matter or form. As LIQUID water, as SOLID water (glaciers, and snow) and as WATER VAPOR or GAS.

The changes in the state of matter is a *physical change* which means that *only the form of water is changing, but not its chemical composition*. All forms of water contain water molecules as two Hydrogen atoms and one Oxygen atom.

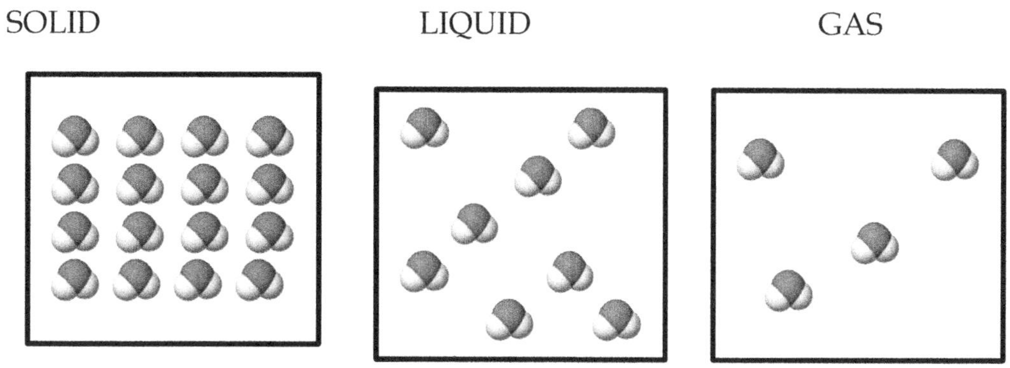

- In a solid form, water molecules are packed tightly and orderly. In a liquid form, the molecules are not held in a particular arrangement and are farther apart compared to the solid form allowing room to flow. Water molecules in the gas form are far away from each other and have high kinetic energy (movement).

Observation Record: My Solar Still

Illustrate:

BEFORE EXPOSING TO SUN

3-4 HRS. LATER UNDER DIRECT SUNLIGHT

Activity A: Water Cycle Foldable

EVAPORATION:
Movement of water as water vapor to air from different water reservoir.

WATER RESERVOIR: An enlarged natural or artificial structure to store water.

PRECIPITATION – Condensed water droplets that fall to the Earth's surface mostly as rain but can also be in the form of sleet, snow, or hail.

CONDENSATION- The transformation of water vapor in the atmosphere into liquid water droplets as clouds or fog.

Activity B: Water Cycle Bead Bracelet

Materials:

Different color beads (dark blue, yellow, clear, white, light blue, green, brown)

Pipe cleaner for each student

Activity Instructions:

- Give each child a pipe cleaner
- Then hand out beads in the following order:
- As you hand-out the beads review the water cycle and ask the child what comes next before giving them the next bead.
    - Dark blue (represents any water reservoir such as ocean, pond or lake)
    - Yellow (Sun)
    - Clear (evaporation)
    - White (clouds- condensation)
    - Light blue (rain- precipitation)
    - Green (vegetation)
    - Brown (ground-run off)
- The student can repeat the cycle until all the pipe cleaner is filled with beads leaving room to tie both ends together. Just make sure that one end starts with dark blue and the other end, end with brown to create a continuous cycle.

Fill in the blanks using the words inside the box to label the parts of the water cycle that the beads represent.

Water Reservoir   Sun
Evaporation (Water vapor)   Clouds
Precipitation (Rain/Snow)   Vegetation   Run-off (ground)

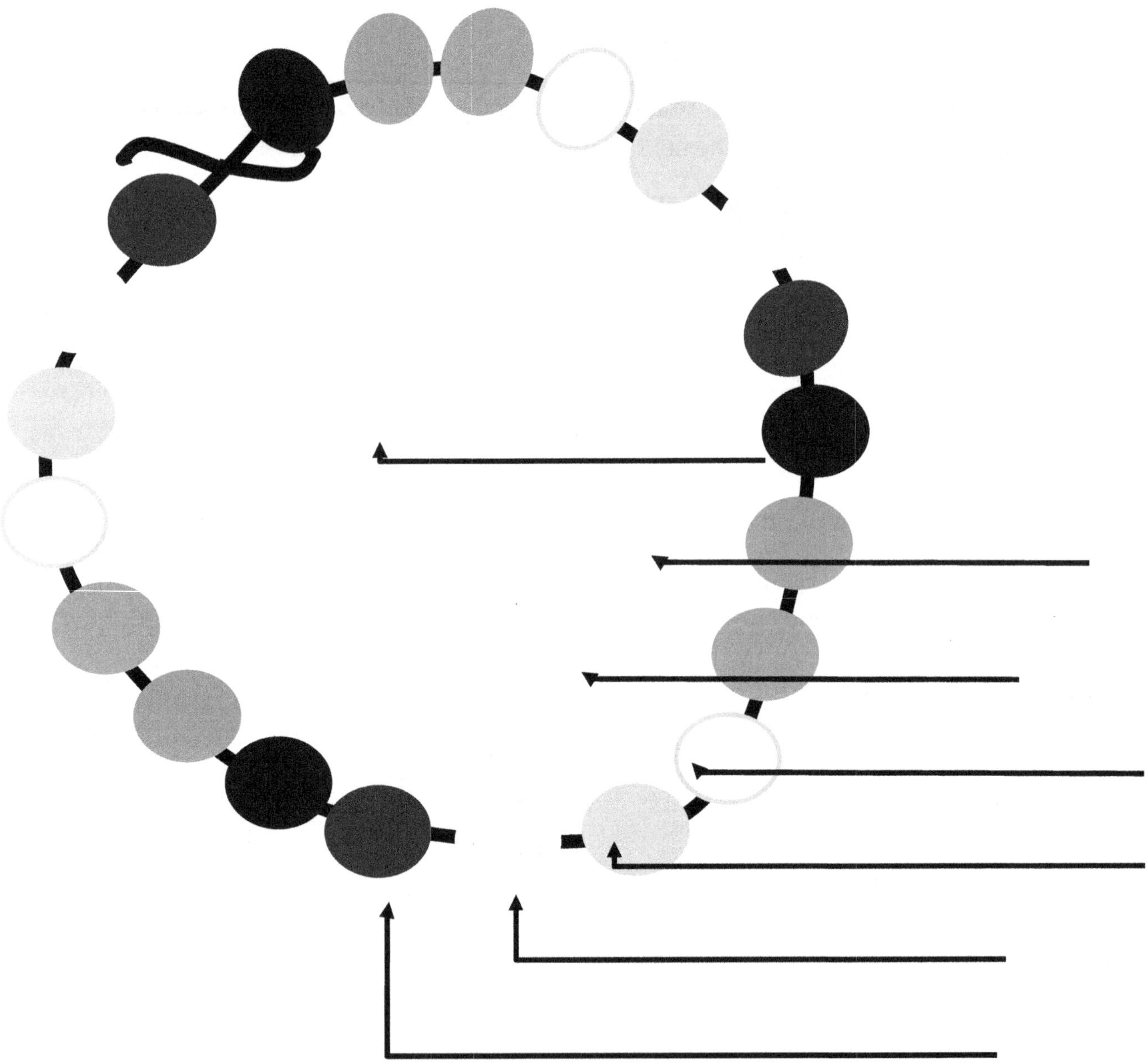

Activity C: Nature Journaling

Location: ______________________________

Date: ______________________________

Unit 22: Surface and Deep Water Ocean Currents

- ☐ LESSON A: Observation and Discussion
    - Read the lesson carefully to make sure you have all needed supplies and you understand the content.
    - Observation Record: Draw what you observed after adding the ice cube, and the red-hot water. Add arrows to show the direction of the movement of water.
- ☐ ACTIVITY A: Focus on Vocabulary
    - The ocean absorbs great amount of heat from the sun and the major ocean current shown below help re-distribute this heat from the Equatorial regions towards the higher latitudes.
    - Color the arrows red to show warm water surface currents and color the arrows blue to show cold water surface currents..
- ☐ ACTIVITY B: Focus on Vocabulary
    - Different marine organisms are affected by ocean currents in their distribution, and migration.
    - Color some of the marine organisms that are affected by ocean currents.
- ☐ PARENT NOTES:

____

____

Lesson A: Surface and Deep Water Ocean Current

Objectives:

3. To demonstrate how different factors such as temperature, salinity, wind and topography affect ocean currents.

Before the Lesson:

- Conduct science outside, whenever possible—check the lesson type and the weather.
- Gather and prep all materials.

Materials Needed:

- ☐ 1 clear container (plastic shoe box or glass dish at last 6 inches deep)
- ☐ Salt
- ☐ Blue food dye
- ☐ Red food dye
- ☐ Ice tray
- ☐ Scotch tape or post-it paper for labeling
- ☐ Marker
- ☐ Hot water
- ☐ Straw* and Clay* (* Extension activities)

In Class:

2. Class Observation:
   - ☐ Ask students to imagine swimming in a pool or a lake.
   - ☐ Now ask the students to think about the water temperature in that pool or lake.
   - ☐ Ask the students if the water towards the top was warmer than the water towards the bottom?
   - ☐ Encourage the students to share why the water temperatures might vary.

     Water on the surface tends to be warmer in a pool or lake due to the heating of the sun.

- Look at "Ocean Currents". Explain to the students that different parts of the world have different water temperatures.

- Ask students to look at the map, and point to the part of the world where they think the water is warmer. Now ask the students to point to the part of the world where they think the water is cooler.

  Water along the Equator is warmer since this part of the Earth gets direct sunlight year- round and as you go higher in latitude towards the North and South Poles, surface water temperature decreases due to the slant angle of the Sun at the poles.

- Explain that when the water moves across the oceans it is called current.

  Currents at the surface of the ocean and currents within the ocean layer results to continuous and directed movement of the ocean water also termed as the great conveyor belt. In this demonstration we will look at how some factors like water temperature, salinity and wind affects ocean currents.

13. Class Activity:

- You can do this as a class demonstration.

- Prior to class: Mix blue food coloring and 2tbsp of salt in 2 cups of water. Freeze the colored salty water in an ice tray.

- Label one end of the tray/dish as "North or South Pole" and the other end as "Equator". Remind the students that the since the equator gets direct sunlight all year round, water in that area is warm. On the other hand, in the polar regions where sunlight hits these areas in an angle, water in the polar regions are colder. In addition, when water freezes making glaciers, the salt in the ocean water remains in solution making the water in the polar regions not only very cold but very salty as well.

- Fill your plastic shoe box or glass dish with tap water.

- Place 3-4 blue ice cubes at one end of the container that is labeled "North or South Pole". Ask the students to observe where the melted blue water goes. Students should observe the blue melted water going down towards the bottom of the container. Have the students draw what they observed.

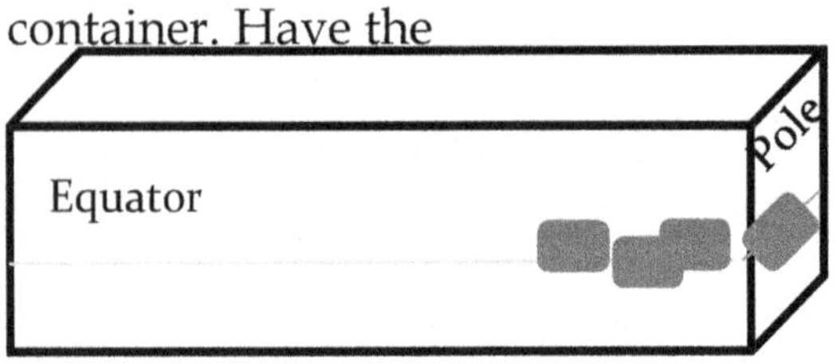

- Place two to three drops of red dye in hot water. Then slowly pour the red, hot water at the "Equator" end. Observe what happens.

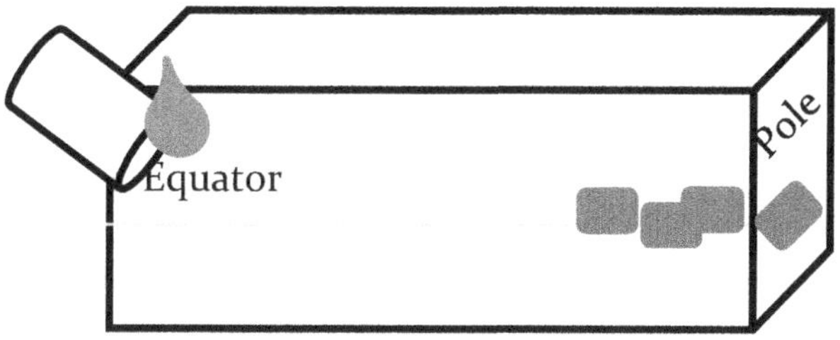

14. Class processing:

a. Have the students look closer at the movement of the cold, blue water and the red, hot water.

b. Where did the cold, blue water go? How about the red, hot water? Did you see the formation of current?

The cold, blue water should sink to the bottom and spread underneath towards the "Equator" side. On the other hand, the red, hot water would be pushed upwards by the cold blue water and move towards the "Pole" side at the surface. This demonstrates how water in the North and South Poles sink to the bottom of the ocean (very cold and salty) and travels towards the equator and resurface there. At the same time, as this happens, the warm water at the equator travels towards the poles and this movement of water creates the "Great Conveyor Belt".

Scientists estimate that it would take 100-1,000 years for a water molecule to complete the circuit of travelling along the conveyor belt.

c. Extension:

Using a straw, ask one of the students to blow gently from the "Equator" side the surface layer of the water. What happened to the circulation? This would represent the strong winds that move water across great expanse e.i. Trade winds and Westerlies that facilitates surface currents.

Topography or the structures seen in the ocean floor like trenches, mountains and valleys can also affect the ocean circulation. You can add these structures by making clay models and placing them at the bottom of the container before adding water. Observe how these structures affect the water circulation.

Observation Record: Ocean Current

After adding the blue ice cube

EQUATOR	POLE

After adding the red-hot water

EQUATOR	POLE

Activity A: Ocean Surface Currents

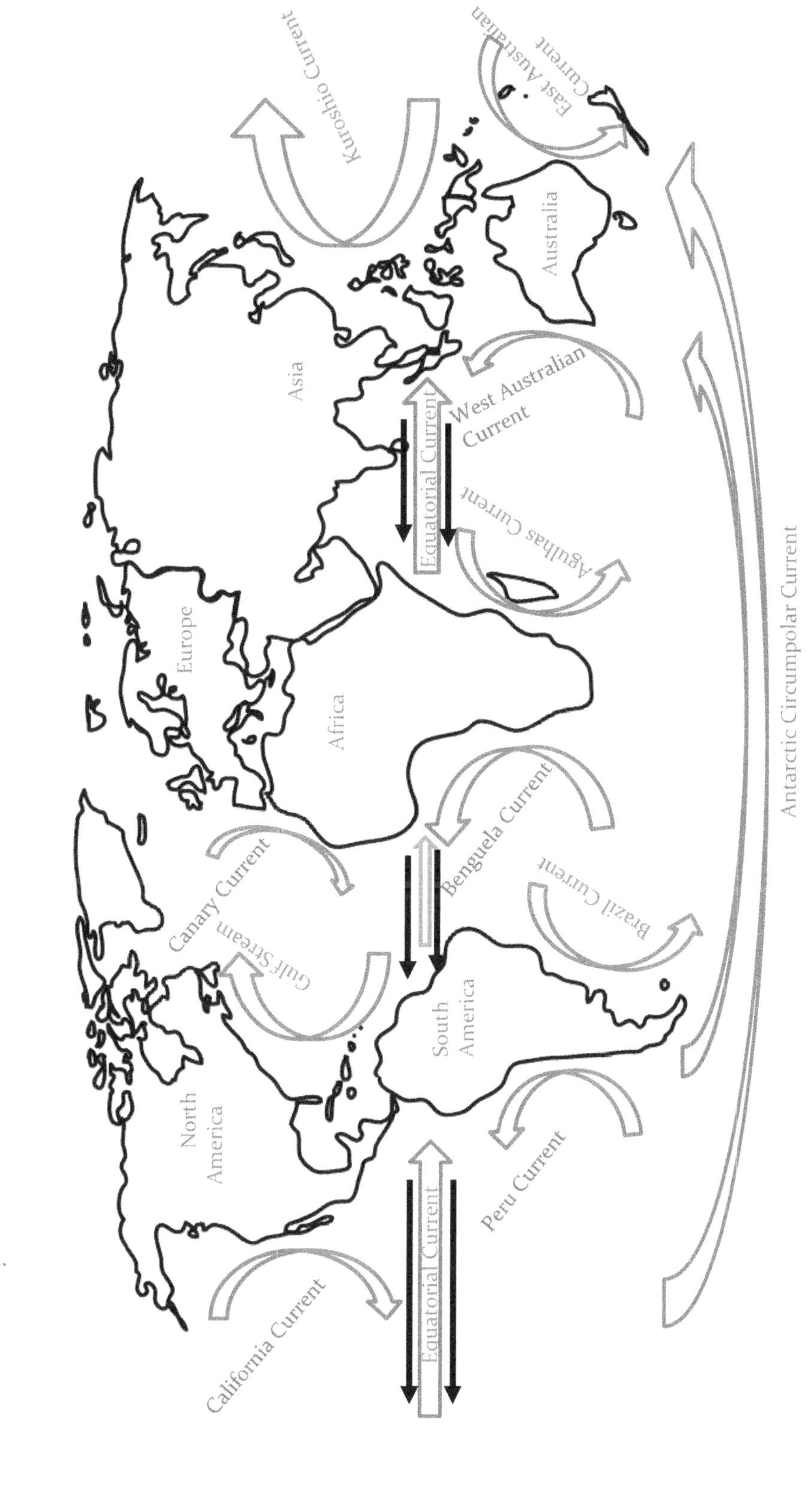

Activity B: Ocean Currents and Marine Organisms

Some organisms like planktons are microscopic 'plants' and 'animals' drift with the currents their entire life.

Invertebrates like jellyfish and other juvenile stages of some marine animals like barnacles, fish eggs and larvae can be subjected to the ocean currents as well at some stage of their life cycle.

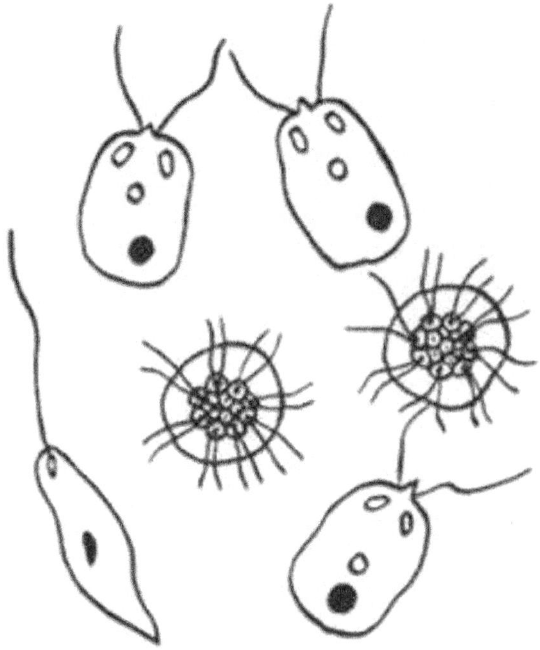

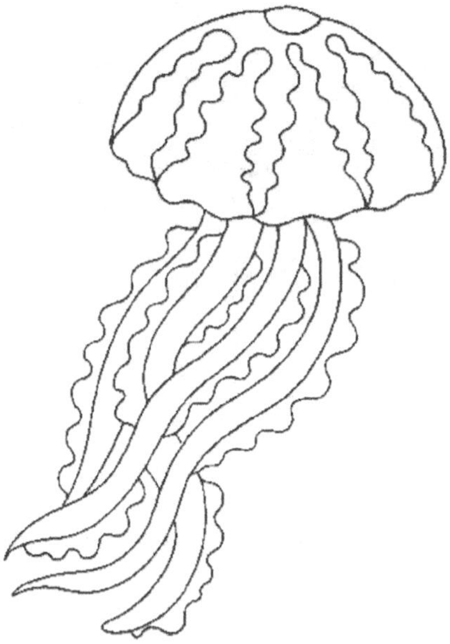

Migration of larger marine organisms such as whales and sea turtles utilized large scale ocean currents that help them travel great distances.

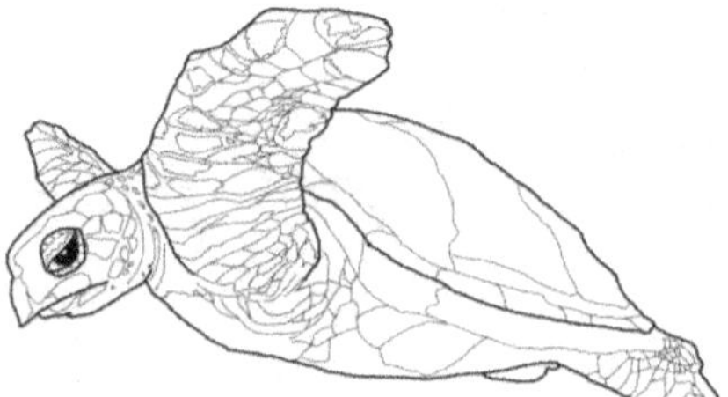

Unit 23: Types of Clouds

- ☐ LESSON A: Observation and Discussion
    - Read the lesson carefully to make sure you have all needed supplies and you understand the content.
    - Observation Record: Cut along the broken lines and glue according to the instructions given in Lesson A.
- ☐ ACTIVITY A: Focus on Vocabulary
    - Gather all the materials listed and make the puffy paint. Use this to make different types of clouds on a blue construction paper as a review.
- ☐ ACTIVITY B: Nature Journaling
    - Lay on the ground and look at the sky. Observe and draw what type of clouds you see. Dictate or write using descriptive words about the clouds you observed.
- ☐ PARENT NOTES:

Lesson A: Types of Clouds

Objective:

This activity provides introduction into the three main types of clouds.

Before the Lesson:

1. Read Science Overview (Handbook) to understand concepts behind this week's lesson.

3. Check the weather before the lesson and decide to conduct the lesson inside or outside.

4. Gather materials for the activity.

Materials Needed:

- ☐ 1 Observation Record "Cloud Types" per student
- ☐ 6 White cotton balls per student
- ☐ 1 Blue construction paper per student
- ☐ 1 Paper plate per student
- ☐ 1 Glue stick per student
- ☐ 1 Pair of scissors per student
- ☐ Hole puncher
- ☐ String or yarn
- ☐ Crayons

In Class:

1. Class Observation:

   ☐ If outside, ask students to look up at the sky at the clouds. If inside, ask the students to think about the clouds they might see in the sky.

   ☐ Review the water cycle and ask the students which part of the water cycle is cloud formation part of. Go over the process of condensation.

   ☐ Explain to the students that there are different types of clouds. The types of clouds can tell you a great deal about the weather.

2. Class Processing & Experiment:

- Pass out the "Cloud Types" Observation Record and ask the students to cut along the broken lines.
- Give one piece of blue construction paper and paper plate per student.
- Instruct the students to glue the sun on the paper plate and the clouds on blue construction paper. Cut along the clouds cut-out. Students can also color the Sun.
- Tell the students that at the back of the clouds cut-out (blue portion), they will create the type of cloud it describes.
- Pass out the cotton balls and instruct students to pull the cotton ball apart to create the different types of cloud.
    - First, create the cirrus cloud. Ask the students to pick the cloud cut-out that has cirrus cloud description on it.
    - Show the students how to make cirrus clouds using cotton balls by reading aloud the description.
    - Glue the cotton ball 'cirrus cloud' at the other side of the cloud cut out.
    - Repeat this step until all the cloud types (Cirrus, Cumulus, and Stratus) have been made
- Cut three holes at the bottom of the paper plate sun and a hole on each cloud cut-out. Using the string or yarn, hang the cloud cut-outs from the sun. Arrange the cloud cut-out to show the different altitudes where each type of cloud is located.
- Punch two holes on top of the Sun paper plate and use it to make a hanger for the "Cloud Types Mobil" that you just created.

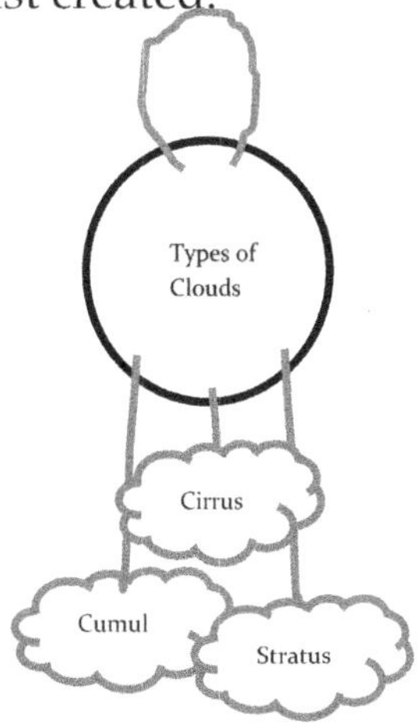

3. Class Discussion:

- What did you learn from this activity?
- How does it help you to understand the sky better?
- Ask students to record the sky everyday for the week as part of their Science Activity.

Types of Clouds

CIRRUS CLOUDS

A high-altitude cloud occurring at 20,000 feet or higher. The Latin word cirrus, meaning a ringlet or curling lock of hair. It is composed of ice crystals from the freezing of super cooled water droplets. Cirrus clouds are characterized by wispy thin strands.

CUMULUS CLOUDS

From the Latin word *Cumulo* meaning "heap" or "pile". Cumulus clouds are often characterized as having fluffy, soft, rounded edges and are cotton ball like in appearance. Normally, cumulus clouds produce little or no precipitation, but they can grow into the precipitation-bearing cumulonimbus.

STRATUS CLOUDS

They are low-lying cloud and appear to be flat, hazy, featureless clouds. They can also appear as grey horizontal layers. Stratus clouds may produce light rain or small amount of snow.

Activity A: Puffy Paint Clouds

Materials:

- ☐ ¾ cup white non-scented shaving cream
- ☐ ¼ cup white glue
- ☐ Bowl for mixing
- ☐ Plastic spoon for mixing
- ☐ Blue construction paper
- ☐ Cotton balls (optional)

Activity:

- ☐ Mix the shaving cream and glue together in a bowl using plastic spoon.
- ☐ Either using your fingers or cotton ball, make the different types of clouds that the student learned from Lesson A by spreading the shaving cream-glue mixture on the blue construction paper.
- ☐ You can also observe the clouds that you see in the sky and ask your student to make the shapes of the clouds he or she observed.
- ☐ Let the puffy paint dry.
- ☐ Once dried, identify the different types of clouds the student painted, and label the clouds as cirrus, cumulus and/or stratus.
- ☐ Have fun with this sensory activity.

Activity B: My Clouds

Date: ________________________________

Location: ______________________________

Unit 24: Types of Weather

☐ LESSON A: Observation and Discussion

- Read the lesson carefully to make sure you have all needed supplies and you understand the content.
- Observation Record: Cut along the broken lines and glue according to the instructions given in Lesson A.

☐ ACTIVITY A: Observations

- Fill in the chart for each day of the week and discuss the overall weather pattern at the end of the week.

☐ ACTIVITY B: Nature Journaling

- Draw and dictate or write using descriptive words about your favorite weather condition. Cut along broken lines and glue to your Weather Lapbook.

☐ PARENT NOTES:

Lesson A: Weather Lapbook

Objective:

This activity provides introduction into the types of weather a meteorologist might use to predict the weather (humidity, atmospheric pressure, precipitation, temperature and, wind speed).

Before the Lesson:

- Check the weather before the lesson and decide to conduct the lesson inside or outside.
- Gather materials for the activity.

Materials Needed:

□ (1) Observation Record "Weather Terms and Instruments" per student

□ (1) File folder per student

□ (3) Pieces of construction paper per student

□ (1) Glue stick per student

□ (1) Set of colored pencils per student

□ (1) Pair of scissors per student.

In Class:

1. Class Observation:

   □ If possible, go outside and ask the student(s) to observe if there is any wind, sunshine, rain, snow outside.

   □ If inside, ask the student(s) to look out the window and make observations about what they see.

2. Class Processing & Experiment:

   □ Pass out one file folder per student.

   □ Tell the student open one file folder and fold each flap in ½, creating 4 equal sections.

   □ Pass out one Observation Record "Weather Terms and Instruments" per student.

- Pass out the construction paper, scissors, glue stick, and tape to the student(s).

- Tell the student(s) to cut out each title and information boxes. They can glue the cut-outs on different colored construction papers to make a back drop.

- Glue one part of the Title box at the left front flap and the other half at the right front flap.

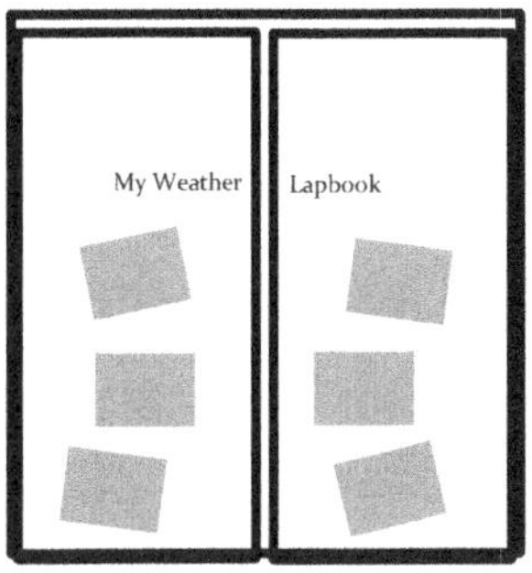

- Glue three of the weather condition pictures on the left front flap and the three on the right front flap. Ask the students to color the pictures of the different weather condition. They can also label these different pictures as sunny, cloudy, partly cloudy, rainy, snowy, and stormy.

- Open the left flap and inside, you can glue the pictures of the different weather instruments. For older students, they can research the functions of the given instruments or research additional weather instruments such as rain gauge or wind vane, and write their descriptions to add in their weather lapbook.

- Open the right flap and inside, students can draw and write about their favorite weather condition (see Activity C).

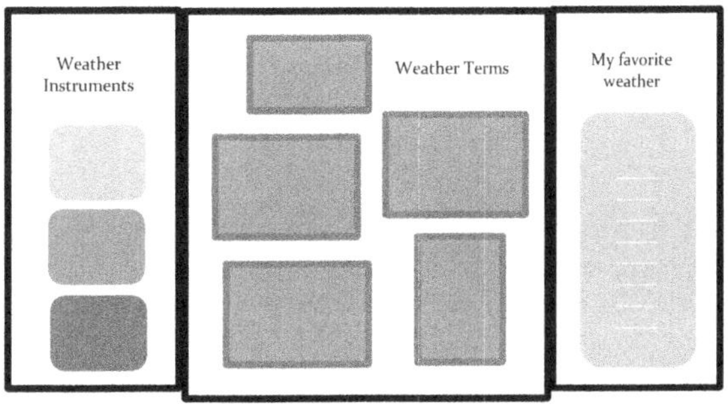

- At the middle of the file folder, glue the different weather terms. Using construction papers, create flaps for each weather terms.

- Encourage the student(s) to be creative with their weather lapbook in their lay-out and designs.

- At the back of the lapbook, you can add pictures of the weather instrument/s the student made and the data table they collected (see Activity A).

3. Class Discussion:

   - What did you learn from this activity?
   - How does it help you to understand the weather.?
   - Encourage the student(s) to share their finished weather lap book.

4. Nature Journaling

   - Ask students to use their lap book to record in their weather observations each day for the next 7 days.

Observation Record: Weather Terms and Instruments

Wind Speed

Wind speed is caused by the movement of air from high to low pressure as a result of change in temperature. The wind speed can be described using Beufort Scale that relates wind speed to observable condition. An anemometer is an instrument to measure wind speed and oftentimes wind direction.

ANEMOMETER

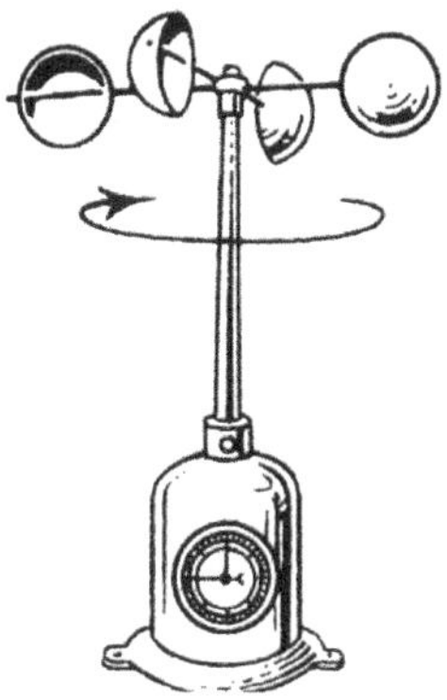

THERMOMETER

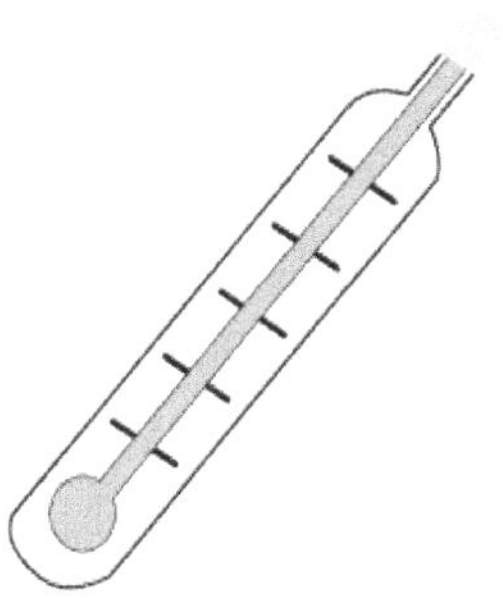

Temperature

Temperature is the amount of heat or cold measured by a thermometer. It is measured in degrees in Celsius, Kelvin, and Fahrenheit. Atmospheric temperature varies by latitude (distance from the equator), altitude (height above the surface of the Earth), season and even change in time (day and night).

Atmospheric Pressure

It is also called Barometric Pressure. It is the measure of the pressure of the weight exerted by the air above a given area on the earth. Atmospheric pressure can be measured by an instrument called a barometer. The average atmospheric pressure is 1 at sea level and decreases with an increase in altitude.

BAROMETER

Humidity
Humidity is the amount of water vapor in the air. More water vapor equals higher humidity.

Precipitation Precipitation is product of condensation of water vapor that falls to the ground. It can be in a form of rain, sleet, hail or snow.

My Weather Lapbook

By: ______________ ______________

Activity A: Weather Charting

	Day 1	Day 2	Day 3	Day 4	Day 5
Types of Clouds					
Temperature					
Wind					

Activity B: My Favorite Weather Condition

My Favorite Weather is ...

Unit 25: The Solar System

- ☐ LESSON A: Observation and Discussion
  - o Read the lesson carefully to make sure you have all needed supplies and you understand the content.
  - o Observation Record: For Teachers: Cut along broken lines and laminate or glue on cardstock. Use this to label the location of the planets and asteroid belt as you unroll the tissue paper.
- ☐ ACTIVITY A: Observations
  - o Gather all the materials listed and make the Outer Space in a Bottle. Use this to play I Spy different planets and other heavenly bodies as a review.
  - o . Color the circles matching the color of the marble you assigned for each planet. Cut and tape on the 'Galaxy Bottle'.
- ☐ ACTIVITY B: Focus on Vocabulary
  - o Trace the words in each box.
- ☐ ACTIVITY C: Nature Journaling
  - o Look at the night sky and observe any heavenly body that you see. Draw what you observe, and dictate or write using descriptive words about what you observed.
- ☐ PARENT NOTES:

____

____

Lesson A: Solar System Model

Objective:

1) To introduce students to the different planets that comprised our solar system.

2) To create a model of the solar system.

3) To investigate the relative distance of the planets from the sun and with another using a model.

Before the Lesson:

- Check the weather before the lesson and decide to conduct the lesson inside or outside.
- Gather materials for the activity.

Materials Needed:

□ (1) Observation Record "Planets of the Solar System" per student

□ (1) Pre-cut and laminated or glued on card stock Observation Record "Planets of the Solar System" per class that will be used during the activity.

□ (2) toilet paper roll (at least 100 sheets per roll) per class or group

□ Crayons or markers

In Class:

1) Class Observation:

□ Ask the students to name some of the heavenly bodies that they see when they look at the night sky.

□ Explain to the students that when they look up at the night sky, they are able to see not only stars, but also planets. Over the years many people have studied the night sky to learn about the planets in our solar system.

2) Class Processing & Experiment:

□ Tell the students that they will learn the different planets that comprised our own solar system.

□ Give students Observation Record "Planets of the Solar System". Go over some facts about each planet. While doing this, students can color the planets.

☐ Tell the students that the size of the planets in their Observation Record are not into scale. To further explain this concept, ask the student to imagine that if the Sun is the size of a basketball (you can bring one and show it to the class), our planet Earth would be only a 2mm dot (you can use a hole punch and use the paper that you punch out to show the relative size of Earth compared to Sun.)

☐ Similarly, ask the students if they can imagine how far the planets are from the Sun and from each other. To better understand the concept of distance that is involve in our solar system, tell that students that the class will make a model using the information in their Observation Record.

☐ The distance of the Earth from the sun is approximately 149,600,000 kilometers (92,957,000 miles). That's a BIG number. Scientists use Astronomical Unit (AU) to make computation of distance easier.

This distance of 149,600,000 kilometers (92,957,000 miles) is equivalent to 1AU. It means that all the planets closer to the sun from Earth has less than 1AU and all the planets farther away from the Earth have greater than 1AU.

Ask the students to look at the Observation Record.

☐ Using toilet paper to measure distance, tell the students that each 10 sheets of the toilet paper is equivalent to 1AU. Place the basketball at one end of a hallway and label it as the sun. Unroll the toilet paper roll, up to 10 sheets and place the pre-cut label for Earth and place it at the end of 10sheets. Place the three planets closer to the Sun using the information in the Observation Record. Continue unrolling the toilet paper roll, asking the students to count as you unroll. Stop and put a planet label every time you reach the correct distance for each planet. Use the Observation Record as a reference.

3. Class Discussion:

☐ What did you learn from this activity?

What can you tell about the distance of terrestrial planets (the first four planets closest to the Sun) relative to the gas planets (the four planets farther away from the Sun).

Observation Record: Planets of the Solar System Facts

	DISTANCE from the SUN	Astronomical Unit (AU)	Toilet paper sheets (1AU=10sheets)	Other Facts
SUN	0	0	Start of the roll	The star at the center of the solar system. Considered as a Yellow Dwarf. One million Earth can fit inside the sun; 109 Earth wide.
MERCURY "The Swift Planet"	35 million miles Or 57 million km	0.4	4 (from the Sun)	Rotation=59 earth days Revolution=88 earth days # of moon= 0 Smallest planet, no atmosphere.
VENUS "The Morning Star" "The evening Star"	67 million miles Or 108 million km	0.7	7 (from the sun)	Rotation=100 earth days Revolution=225 earth days # of moon= 0 Atmosphere mostly carbon dioxide, on the average the hottest planet
EARTH "The Ocean Planet" "The Blue Planet"	93 million miles Or 150 million km	1.0	10 (from the sun)	Rotation=1 day Revolution=365 days # of moon= 1 The only planet that has breathable air, liquid water and presence of life.

MARS "The Red Planet"	142 million miles Or 228 million km	1.5	15 (from the sun)	Rotation=1 day and 37mins Revolution=687 earth days or 1.9 years # of moon= 2 Atmosphere mostly carbon dioxide, has massive volcanoes.
Asteroid Belt		2.8	28 (from the sun)	Resides between the orbit of Mars and Jupiter. Made of rocks (billions of asteroids). The four largest asteroids are named Ceres, Vesta, Phallas and Hygiea (they contain half the mass of the entire belt).
JUPITER Known for its "Red Spot" or also called the "Eye of Jupiter" "The Giant Planet"	484 million miles Or 779 million km	5.2	52 (from the sun)	Rotation=9 hrs 55 mins Revolution=4,332 Earth days or 11.86 years # of moon= 50 The largest planet (1,300 Earth can fit inside), has rings, atmosphere has poisonous gas.
SATURN "The Ringed Planet"	889 million miles Or 1.43 billion km	9.6	96 (from the sun)	Rotation= 10 hrs Revolution= 29.5 years # of moon= at least 18 moons The second largest planet, known for its rings that are made of ice crystals.

URANUS "The Ice Giant Planet"	1.79 billion miles Or 2.88 billion km	19.2	192 (from the sun)	Rotation=17.9 hrs Revolution=84 Earth years # of moon= 27 Rotates sideways, atmosphere has high methane gas content, has 13 rings.
NEPTUNE "The Big Blue Planet"	2.8 billion miles Or 4.5 billion km	30.0	300 (from the sun)	Rotation=16 hrs 6 mins Revolution=165 Earth years # of moon= 14 Atmosphere mostly hydrogen, helium and methane, has 6 rings, on average considered the coldest planet.

Inner Planets or Terrestrial Planets

Outer Planets or Gas Planets

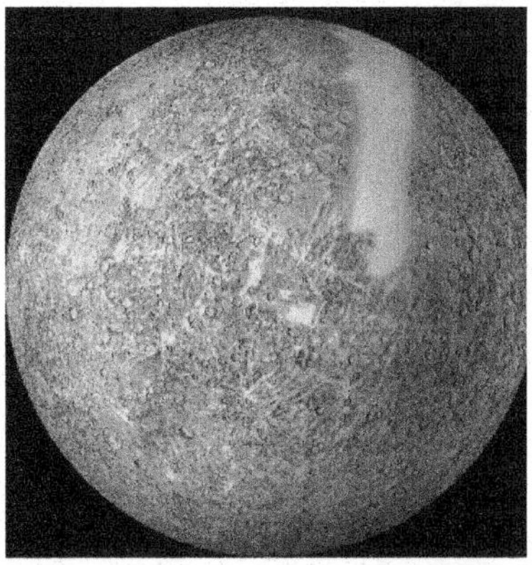

Mercury

Venus

Earth

https://www.wpclipart.com/space/solar_system/mercury.png.html
https://www.wpclipart.com/space/solar_system/Venus/Venus_UV_image.jpg.html
https://www.wpclipart.com/space/solar_system/Earth/globes_2/globe.png.html

Mars

Jupiter

Saturn

https://www.wpclipart.com/space/solar_system/Mars/Mars_from_Viking_large.jpg.html

https://www.wpclipart.com/space/solar_system/Jupiter/Jupiter_isolated.png.html

https://www.wpclipart.com/space/solar_system/Saturn/Saturn_Hubble.jpg.html

Uranus

Neptune

Asteroid Belt

https://www.wpclipart.com/space/solar_system/uranus.png.html
https://www.wpclipart.com/space/solar_system/Neptune/Neptune.jpg.html
https://www.wpclipart.com/space/asteroid/asteroid_ida_1993_by_Galileo_spacecraft.png.html

Activity A: Outer Space in a Bottle

Materials:

- ☐ Water plastic bottle
- ☐ Mineral or Baby oil
- ☐ Water
- ☐ Blue and red dye
- ☐ 8 different color marbles to represent different planets, 1 big marble for the Sun
- ☐ Small rocks to represent asteroids
- ☐ Clear tape
- ☐ Glow in the dark plastic stars (optional)
- ☐ Glitter (optional)

Activity:

- ☐ Assign a marble for a planet and color the I Spy Label, matching the color of the marble to the planet.
- ☐ Mix the blue and red dye in 1 cup water until you end up with a dark purple mixture.
- ☐ Place your marbles, pebbles, stars and glitter inside the water bottle.
- ☐ Fill the water bottle half-way with the mineral or baby oil.
- ☐ Then, pour the water-food dye mixture until the water bottle is full.
- ☐ Screw the cap tightly making sure the liquid inside is not leaking.
- ☐ Seal the cap with tape.
- ☐ Tape the I Spy Label at one side of the bottle.
- ☐ Shake the bottle and find the different 'Planets' inside your 'Galaxy in a Bottle'.

I Spy Label:

I Spy....
- Mercury ○
- Venus ○
- Earth ○
- Mars ○
- Jupiter ○
- Saturn ○
- Uranus ○
- Neptune ○
- Asteroids
- Sun ○
- Stars ☆

I Spy....
- Mercury ○
- Venus ○
- Earth ○
- Mars ○
- Jupiter ○
- Saturn ○
- Uranus ○
- Neptune ○
- Asteroids
- Sun ○

Activity B: Solar System Writing Practice

Mercury

Venus

Earth

https://www.wpclipart.com/space/solar_system/mercury.png.html
https://www.wpclipart.com/space/solar_system/Venus/Venus_UV_image.jpg.html
https://www.wpclipart.com/space/solar_system/Earth/globes_2/globe.png.html

Mars

Jupiter

Saturn

https://www.wpclipart.com/space/solar_system/Mars/Mars_from_Viking_large.jpg.html

https://www.wpclipart.com/space/solar_system/Jupiter/Jupiter_isolated.png.html
https://www.wpclipart.com/space/solar_system/Saturn/Saturn_Hubble.jpg.html

Uranus

Neptune

Asteroid

https://www.wpclipart.com/space/solar_system/uranus.png.html
https://www.wpclipart.com/space/solar_system/Neptune/Neptune.jpg.html

https://www.wpclipart.com/space/asteroid/asteroid_ida_1993_by_Galileo_spacecraft.png.html

Moon

Comet

Galaxy

https://www.wpclipart.com/space/moon/moon_lithograph.jpg.html
https://www.wpclipart.com/space/comet/ISON/comet_ison_may8_hubble.jpg.html
https://www.wpclipart.com/space/stars_universe/galaxy/spiral_galaxy_M81_in_ultraviolet.jp
g.html

Activity C: Nature Journaling

Date: ___________________________________

Location: _________________________________

____

____

____

____

____

____

____

____

____

____

____

____

Unit 26: More About the Solar System

- ☐ LESSON A: Observation and Discussion
  - o Read the lesson carefully to make sure you have all needed supplies and you understand the content.
- ☐ ACTIVITY A: Focus on Vocabulary
  - o Scavenger Hunt Observation Record: Put a check mark (/) once you find the matching card.
  - o Fact Cards to Find: Cut along broken lines and laminate or glue on cardstock. Hide in various places in your classroom and have students check off in their Observation Record when they find a card that matches.
- ☐ ACTIVITY B: Focus on Vocabulary
  - o Cut the pictures of METEOROID, METEOR and METEORITES and paste the pictures in their right locations.
- ☐ ACTIVITY C: Nature Journaling
  - o Look at the night sky and observe any heavenly body that you see. Draw what you observe, and dictate or write using descriptive words about what you observed.
- ☐ PARENT NOTES:

____

____

Lesson A: 'Small Bodies' of the Solar System Model

Objective:

1) To introduce students to other heavenly bodies that comprised our solar system.
2) To create a model of some of these 'small bodies' of the solar system.

Before the Lesson:

- Check the weather before the lesson and decide to conduct the lesson inside or outside.
- Gather materials for the activity.

Materials Needed:

- ☐ 4-6 cups of mashed potatoes (can also use boxed mashed potato).
- ☐ ¼ - ½ cup butter
- ☐ Salt and pepper
- ☐ Mixing bowl
- ☐ Spoon
- ☐ Baking dish or sheet
- ☐ 6x6 foil or parchment paper
- ☐ Oven

In Class:

1) Class Observation:

   - ☐ Ask the students besides the stars and the planets, what other heavenly bodies are found in our solar system?

   Besides stars and planets, one can also find other materials that orbits the Sun or other planets.

   a) *Moons-Moons are natural satellites that orbit planets and asteroids in our solar system. To date, there are 203 moon that orbits around various planets in our solar system. Moons are not necessarily spherical in shape. They come in various sizes, shapes and composition.*

b) *Asteroids- Sometimes called as ancient rubbles, asteroids are rocky heavenly bodies that too small to be considered planets. They can be as small as a few meters to hundreds of kilometers long. Scientist believed that they are remnants of rocks during the early formation of the solar system that didn't come together to form the planets we know today. Currently there are close to 800,000 known asteroids and most of them are located between Mars and Jupiter. This area is commonly called the asteroid belt.*

c) *Comets- Comets are made up of frozen water, gases, rocks and dusts and some organic materials. The nucleus of the comet is the head of the comet. When a comet gets close to the Sun, parts of the nucleus outgas forming the corona that surrounds the nucleus. The tails of the comet are created due to the effect of the solar radiation and wind. As a result, the tails point away from the Sun. Comets revolve around the sun in an elliptical orbit. There are about 3,500 known comets.*

d) *Meteoroids, Meteors and Meteorites- The term <u>meteoroids</u> refer to small 'space rocks' that can be from fragments of asteroids; when these meteoroids enter the Earth's atmosphere and burn up sometimes creating streak of lights in the atmosphere, it is called <u>meteors</u>; when the meteors survived Earth's atmosphere and hit the ground, the remnants of these 'space rocks' are called <u>meteorites</u>.*

- Show students pictures of the small heavenly bodies discussed above as you describe each one of them.

2) Class Processing & Experiment:

- Tell the students that they will create a model of an asteroid.
- Talk about the different shapes of asteroid and what they look like.
- Tell them that asteroids can be as big as a school bus but we are just making a tiny one which a size that can also be found in outer space.
- Mixed the butter, salt and pepper with the mashed potato. Ask a volunteer to mix and volunteers to add the other ingredients.
- Once all the ingredients are mixed, give each student foil or parchment paper that has been pre-cut.
- Divide the mashed potato among the students and asked them to shape it like an asteroid and put dents or craters using their fingers. Once done, ask the students to place their 'potato asteroid' on the foil/parchment paper and arrange them on a baking sheet.
- Place the 'potato asteroid' inside the oven at 357°F for 20 minutes or until golden brown, then serve and enjoy!

Activity A: Solar System Scavenger Hunt

Objective:

To learn new terms and review terms and facts that pertain to the study of Astronomy.

Before the Lesson:

- Check the weather before the lesson and decide to conduct the lesson inside or outside.
- Gather materials for the activity.

Materials Needed:

- ☐ (1) Observation Record " Solar System Scavenger Hunt" per student
- ☐ (15) Solar System Fact Cards per class
- ☐ Tape
- ☐ Small prize for finishing the scavenger hunt

In Class:

- ☐ Prior to class copy or use the Solar System Fact Cards, laminate or glue them on card stocks. Place them all around the classroom or outside if the weather is nice.
- ☐ Review the lesson last week.
- ☐ Tell the students that they will go on a scavenger hunt.
- ☐ Give each student an Observation Record "Solar System Scavenger Hunt", and tell the students that they have to find the answers to the clues in their Observation Record by looking for 15 "Solar System Fact Cards" that you placed in various places in your classroom or in the yard.
- ☐ Go over the answers as a class and give a small prize for finishing the scavenger hunt.
- ☐ Children who can read can pair up with non-reader students to do the scavenger hunt.

Observation Record: Solar System Scavenger Hunt

Mercury ○

Venus ○

Earth ○

Mars ○

Jupiter ○

Saturn ○

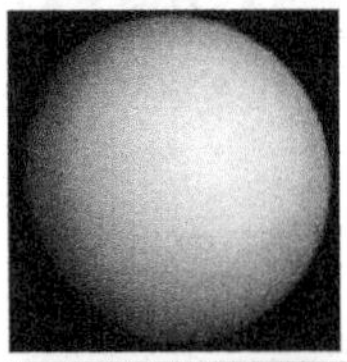
Uranus ○

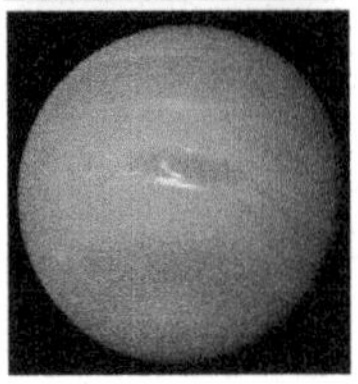
Neptune ○

https://www.wpclipart.com/space/solar_system/mercury.png.html
https://www.wpclipart.com/space/solar_system/Venus/Venus_UV_image.jpg.html
https://www.wpclipart.com/space/solar_system/Earth/globes_2/globe.png.html
https://www.wpclipart.com/space/solar_system/Mars/Mars_from_Viking_large.jpg.html
https://www.wpclipart.com/space/solar_system/Jupiter/Jupiter_isolated.png.html
https://www.wpclipart.com/space/solar_system/Saturn/Saturn_Hubble.jpg.html
https://www.wpclipart.com/space/solar_system/uranus.png.html
https://www.wpclipart.com/space/solar_system/Neptune/Neptune.jpg.html
https://www.wpclipart.com/space/asteroid/asteroid_ida_1993_by_Galileo_spacecraft.png.html

Mercury

Venus

Earth

Mars

Jupiter

Saturn

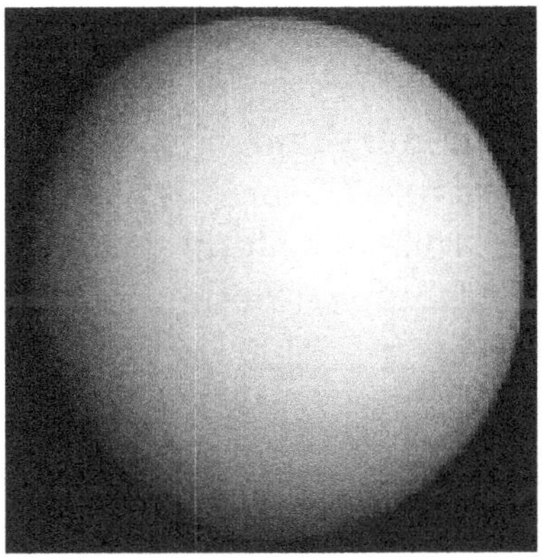

Uranus

Neptune

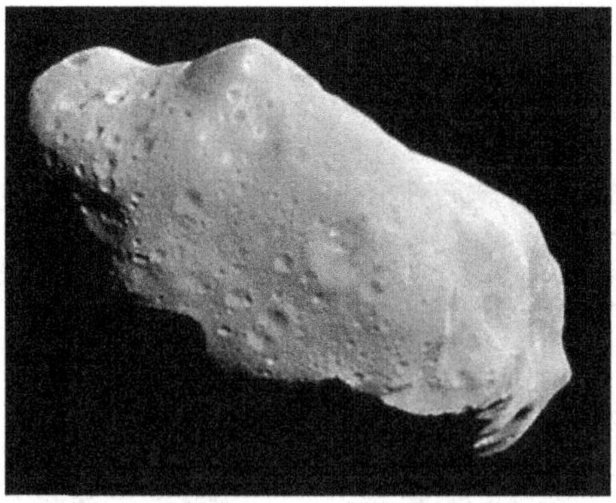

Asteroid Belt

Sun

https://www.wpclipart.com/space/solar_system/mercury.png.html
https://www.wpclipart.com/space/solar_system/Venus/Venus_UV_image.jpg.html
https://www.wpclipart.com/space/solar_system/Earth/globes_2/globe.png.html
https://www.wpclipart.com/space/solar_system/Mars/Mars_from_Viking_large.jpg.html
https://www.wpclipart.com/space/solar_system/Jupiter/Jupiter_isolated.png.html
https://www.wpclipart.com/space/solar_system/Saturn/Saturn_Hubble.jpg.html
https://www.wpclipart.com/space/solar_system/uranus.png.html
https://www.wpclipart.com/space/solar_system/Neptune/Neptune.jpg.html
https://www.wpclipart.com/space/asteroid/asteroid_ida_1993_by_Galileo_spacecraft.png.html

Activity B: Meteoroids, Meteors, and Meteorites

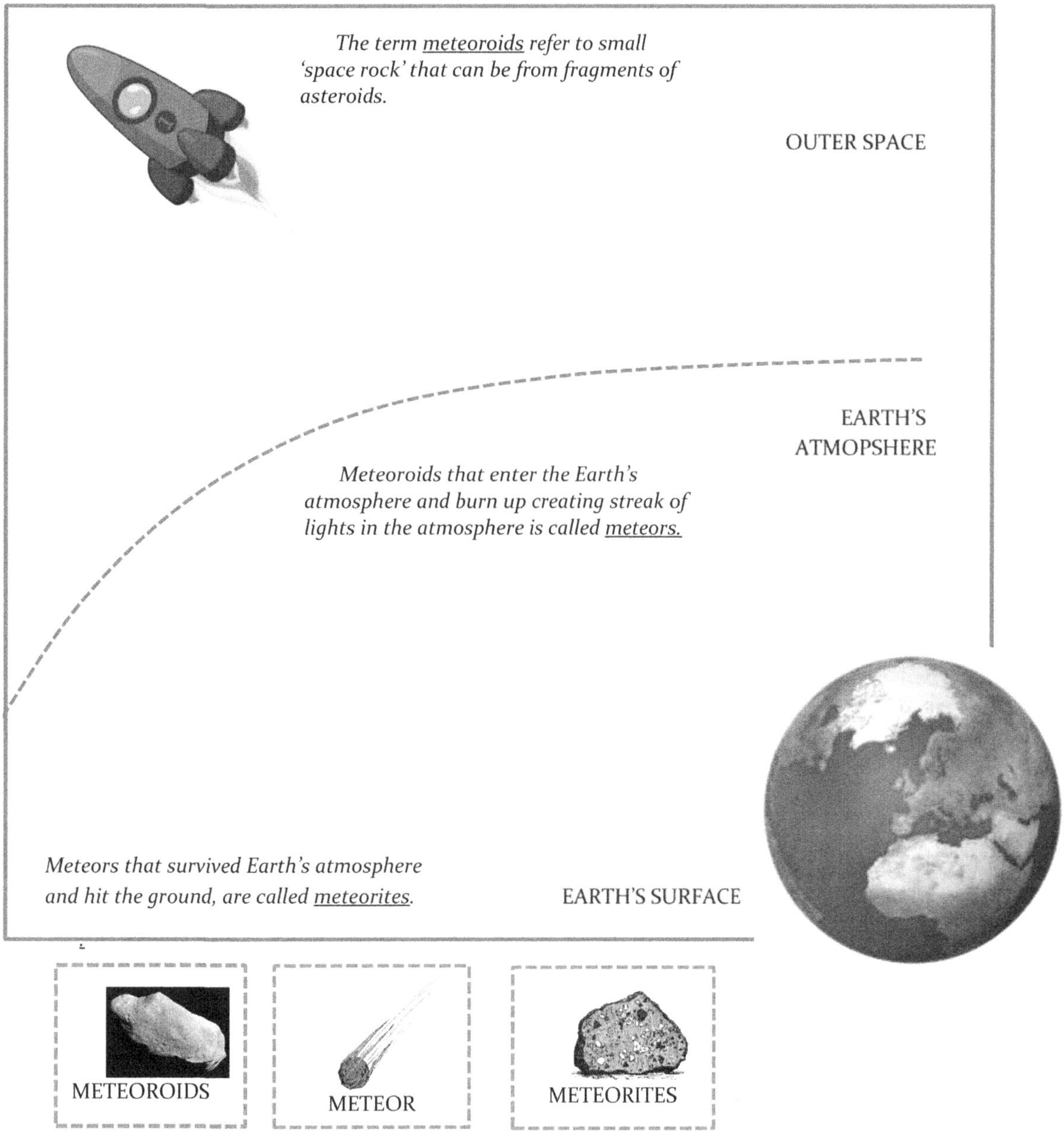
The term meteoroids refer to small 'space rock' that can be from fragments of asteroids.
OUTER SPACE
EARTH'S ATMOPSHERE
Meteoroids that enter the Earth's atmosphere and burn up creating streak of lights in the atmosphere is called meteors.
Meteors that survived Earth's atmosphere and hit the ground, are called meteorites.
EARTH'S SURFACE
METEOROIDS
METEOR
METEORITES

Activity C: Nature Journaling

Date: ________________________________

Location: ________________________________

Unit 27: Earth's Rotation & Revolution

- ☐ LESSON A: Observation and Discussion
    - Read the lesson carefully to make sure you have all needed supplies and you understand the content.
- ☐ ACTIVITY A: Focus on Vocabulary
    - Complete this hands-on activity with your student.
- ☐ ACTIVITY B: Focus on Vocabulary
    - Cut the pictures of the Earth and glue each of them to correspond to the right season (for the Northern Hemisphere) as the Earth revolves around the sun..
- ☐ ACTIVITY C: Nature Journaling
    - Pick a season and, inside the box draw your favorite activity during that time of the year. Describe your picture by writing or dictating your description to your parent.
- ☐ PARENT NOTES:

____

____

Lesson A: Earth's Rotation and Revolution

Objective:

In this activity, students will pretend to be planets to demonstrate both the rotation and revolution movements of planets.

Before the Lesson:

- Check the weather before the lesson and decide to conduct the lesson inside or outside.
- Gather materials for the activity.

Materials Needed:

- ☐ Observation Record "Rotation and Revolution of the Earth" per student
- ☐ Any light source (candle, lantern or flashlight)
- ☐ Chalk to make orbit
- ☐ Writing materials
- ☐ Coloring pencils or crayons

In-Class:

1. Class Observation:

   ☐ Invite the students to sit in a semicircle around you.

   ☐ Review the information learned in the previous lesson.

   ☐ Ask the students to tell you the two ways the Earth moves.

2. Class Activity:

   ☐ Before class, pick a room that has a large and open space or you can also do this activity outdoors. Using a chalk, you can draw a large circle on the floor that would represent an orbit.

   ☐ Ask the students if they know the names of two types of movements the Earth makes. (*rotation and revolution*).

   ☐ To explain this concept put the source of light you brought in the middle of the big circle you drew earlier.

- Ask everyone to stand around the source of light stepping on the circle you drew. This will be a good time to review how planets are located around the Sun and the Sun is the center of our Solar System.
- Tell the students that each one of them will imagine themselves as a planet. Planet moves on its axis and this movement of planets is called rotation. Most planets rotate from West to East or in a counterclockwise rotation. Ask the students who can remember which two planets rotate in the opposite direction and one that rotates 'lying down'. *The answer is Venus and Uranus.*
- Have students spin in a counterclockwise direction not leaving where they are standing. Maybe you can ask couple of students to rotate clockwise to represent Venus and Uranus. Try only 3-4 spins to avoid getting dizzy.
- Next, tell the students that planets not only rotate on their axes, they also move around the Sun and this movement is called revolution.
- This time, ask the students to move around the Sun. Remind students that planets stay in their orbits while revolving around the Sun so they should also maintain their distance from the Sun by staying on the circle you drew. Try 2-3 revolution around the source of light.
- Lastly, tell the students that when planets move around the Sun, they rotate on their axes at the same time. Ask the students to do the same. Have them spin while revolving around the source of light. Some of your students might spin slower than the others. Remind the students that planets are the same. Some planets revolve around the Sun and spins faster on their axes compared to the other ones.
- If you have time, have students work on the Observation Record: "Earth's Rotation and Revolution." Students can finish the record at home.

3. Class Discussion:

   - When you are spinning, can you see the sun at all times? *No, because there are times when you are facing away from the sun.*
   - What does rotation mean in terms of time? *The rotation of the Earth represents one day or 24hrs. The time when you are facing the sun represents daytime and the time when you are facing away from the sun represents nigh time.*
   - What does the revolution in terms of time means? *The revolution of the Earth around the sun represents one year or 365 ¼ days. You can discuss the reason here why we have leap years.*
   - *The position of the sun around the sun bring about the different seasons in a year.*

Activity A: Model of Earth's Rotation and Revolution

Objective:

In this activity, students will be creating paper models of the Earth's rotation.

Materials Needed:

- (2) Brad clips per student
- (1) Pair of scissors per student
- (1) Glue stick per student
- (1) Set of colored pencils per student
- (1) sheet of paper or Science Journals for recording.

Class Activity:

- Tell the students to color the Moon, the Earth, and the Sun.
- Next, students will cut out all the parts.
- Attach the brad by poking a hole into the image where the dots are located.
- By connecting the Earth to the sun this represents the Earth revolving around the sun.
- Next, attach the second brad to represent the Earth turning on its axis.
- Lastly, attach the moon to the second brad to represent how the moon revolves around the Earth.
- Encourage students to turn the earth slowly in a circle by moving just the Earth.
- Now, ask the students to move the Earth around the sun while rotating the Earth.
- Finally, have the students move the moon around the Earth. Then, try and move all three at the same time.
- Allow the students to work quietly and give assistance as needed.

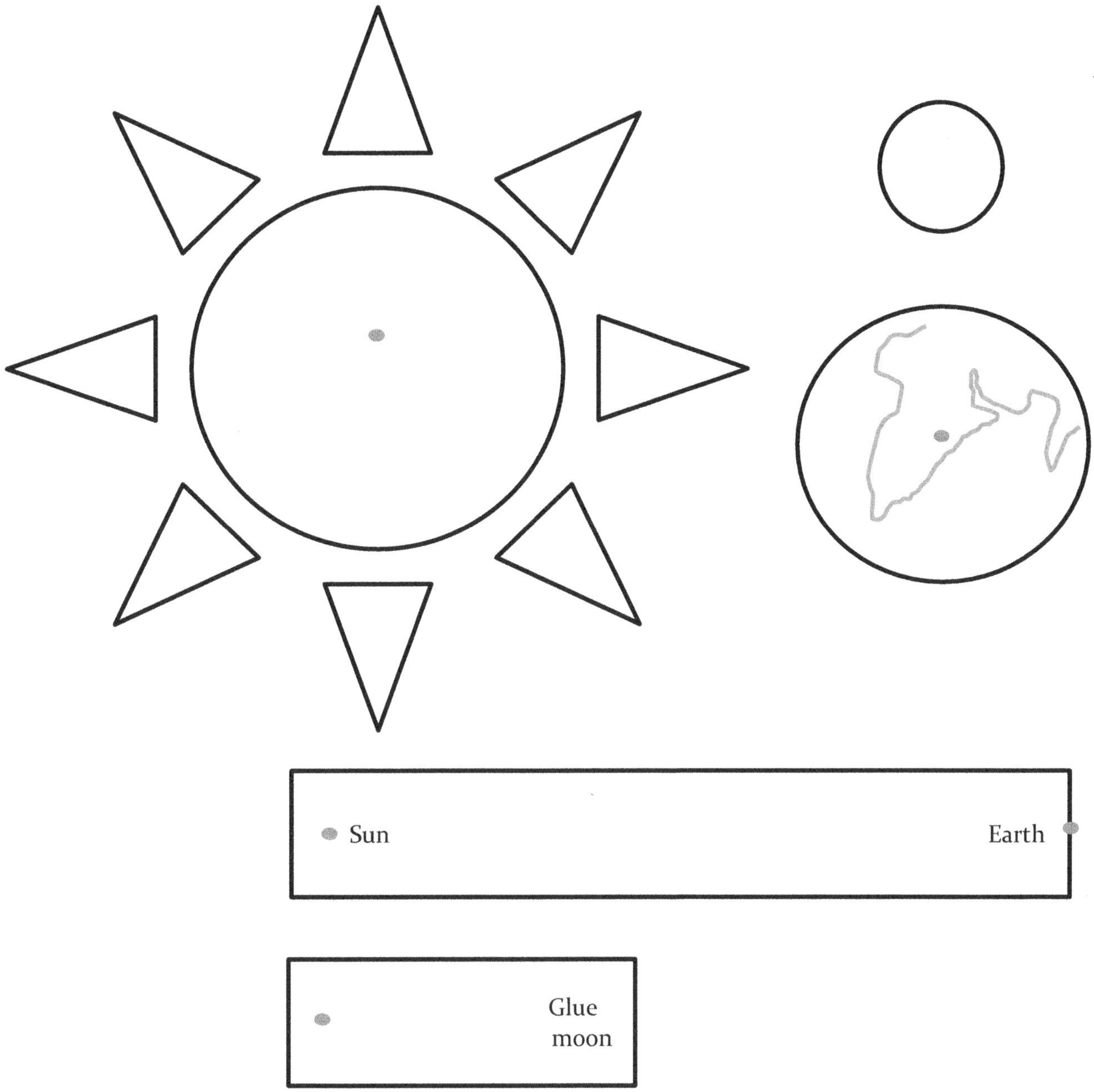
Sun
Earth
Glue
moon

Activity B: Reasons for the Season

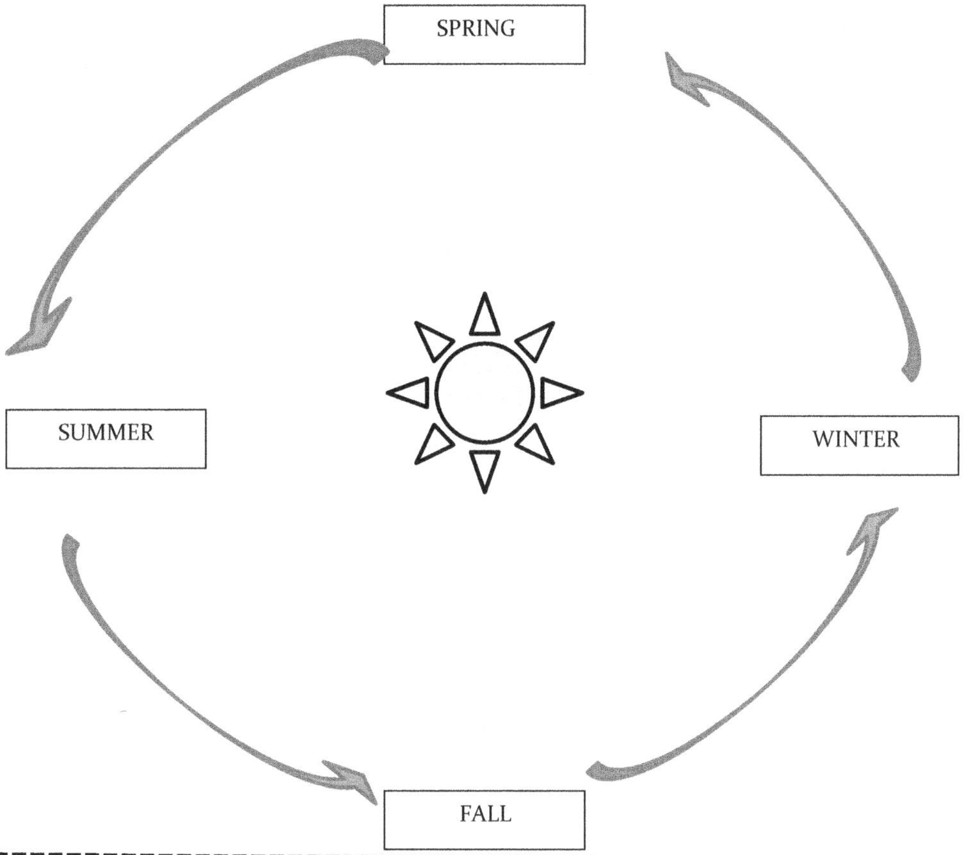

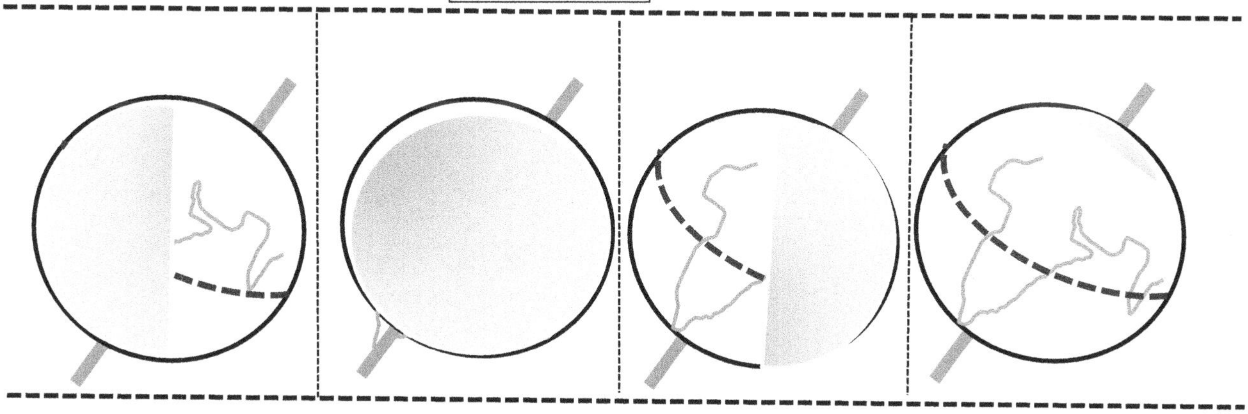

Four Seasons

The revolution of the Earth around the Sun takes 365 ¼ days which is equivalent to one year. On a regular year, we have only 365 days. So, what happened to the quarter day

(6hrs)? The 6 hours is added and on the fourth year, we add one day (6hrs x 4= 24 hrs) in our calendar year resulting to a leap year.

SUMMER in the Northern Hemisphere occurs on June 20 or 21st also known as the summer solstice. On this day the sun is at its highest point in the Northern Hemisphere sky at noon and experienced the longest daylight in the year. Since the earth is tilted at a 23.5°angle, during these months, the Northern Hemisphere is tilted towards the sun while the Southern Hemisphere is tilted away from the sun and therefore, receives the sun's rays at an angle. As a result, it is summer in the Northern Hemisphere and winter in the Southern Hemisphere.

FALL or AUTUMN in the Northern Hemisphere begins on September 22 or 23 when the Earth is not tilted toward or away from the sun. On this day, the length of day and night are equal (12 hours each) all over the Earth. This day is known as the equinox. It is Spring in the Southern Hemisphere.

WINTER in the Northern Hemisphere occurs on December 21 or 22 also known as the winter solstice. Since the earth is tilted at a 23.5°angle, during these months, the Northern Hemisphere is tilted away from the sun while the Southern Hemisphere is tilted towrads the sun and therefore, receives the longest amount of daylight. As a result, it is winter in the Northern Hemisphere and summer in the Southern Hemisphere.

SPRING in the Northern Hemisphere begins March 20 or 21 when again the Earth is not tilted toward or away from the sun. There are 12 hours of daylight and 12 hours of darkness on this day. It is Fall in the Southern Hemisphere

Activity C: Nature Journaling

Date: ______________________________

Location: ______________________________

Unit 28: Types of Stars

☐ LESSON A: Observation and Discussion

- Read the lesson carefully to make sure you have all needed supplies and you understand the content.

☐ ACTIVITY A: Focus on Vocabulary

- Complete this hands-on activity with your student.

☐ ACTIVITY B: Focus on Vocabulary

- Color the different stages in the life cycle of star.
- Color the Stellar Nebula - Purple, Average Star - Yellow, Red Giant - Red, Planetary Nebula - Dark Blue and White Dwarf - White, Massive Star - Light Blue, Red Supergiant - Red Orange, Supernova - White, Neutron Star - Yellow and Black Hole - Black.

☐ ACTIVITY C: Nature Journaling

- On a cloudless night, observe the night sky from when you spotted a star. Draw what you observe. Looking at the same area where you spotted the first star, draw the stars you see every hour for three hours.

☐ PARENT NOTES:

____

____

____

____

Lesson A: Types of Stars

*This activity was adapted from Mary Kay Hemenway, University of Texas at Austin

Objective:

In this activity, students will look into the different types of stars based on color and size.

Before the Lesson:

- Check the weather before the lesson and decide to conduct the lesson inside or outside.
- Gather materials for the activity.

Materials Needed:

- ☐ Observation Record "Types of Stars: Colors"
- ☐ Candle and candle holder
- ☐ Match or lighter
- ☐ Crayons or colored pencils

In-Class:

4. Class Observation:
   - ☐ Invite the students to sit in a semicircle around you.
   - ☐ Review the information learned in the previous lesson.
   - ☐ Ask the students what they know about stars.
   - ☐ Do they know what it is made of? Can they student describe what a star looks like?
   - ☐ Tell the students that our Sun is a type of star.

     Our Sun is made up mostly of Hydrogen and Helium. We can describe the Sun as a big ball of hot gas.

     It looks really big compared to the other stars in the night sky, but it is actually not the biggest star in our galaxy. It looks big because it is the closest star to us. You can read additional facts about our Sun using reference books.

5. Class Activity:
    a. Ask the students what do they think is the color of our Sun? Most students probably will respond as yellow. Tell the students that not all stars are yellow. Some come in a different color besides yellow.
    b. Tell the students that they will observe a flame from a candle and they will try to see the different color of the flame that the candle produce.
    c. Give them the Observation Record and crayons/coloring pencils and ask them to color the flame in their Observation Record using the color/s they see on the flame.
    d. You can also take pictures of the flame and have the students look at the picture for observation of the colors as well.
6. Class Discussion:
    a. Ask the students the different color they observe.
    b. Which color is the middle of the flame? Which color did they see on the edge of the flame?

       The middle of the flame would appear more whitish or bluish while the outer edge would appear more orange or reddish. Tell the students that just like the hottest part of the flame that appears bluish-white, the hottest star is also color blue and white (Class O and has a temperature as high as 50,000K). On the other end, the "coldest" stars (which still have much higher temperature than any materials on Earth), are color red (Class M, with temperature of 2,500-3,500K) which is the color we see at the outer edge of the flame. The sun is a yellow star which has intermediate temperature (Class G with temperature of 5,000-6,000K.)

       **1 ° Fahrenheit (F) = 255.93 Kelvin (K)*

       The color that the scientists observed when they categorize stars is based on the temperature of the outermost layer of the star. This layer is called the photosphere.
    c. Ask the students if they've seen a metal being heated up. At first it will appear red but as you continue to heat up the metal, it will change its color to yellowish then white which reflects the hottest temperature of the metal similar to stars.

Activity A: Build a Sundial

As the Earth rotates in its axis, the Sun's position in the sky changes with time causing objects to cast shadow as the Sun 'moves'. A sundial is made of thin rod also called a gnomon that casts a shadow. The location of the shadow changes throughout the day reflecting the passing of time. In this activity, students will be creating a sundial to tie in lesson about Earth's rotation and the time of the day with respect to the position of the Sun in the sky.

Materials Needed:

- ☐ White paper plate
- ☐ Pencil or stick
- ☐ Clay
- ☐ Compass
- ☐ Marker
- ☐ Watch with alarm

Activity:

- ☐ This activity is best done on a cloudless day. Pick a spot in your yard or an open space where there is no obstruction or object that can cause to cast a shadow on your sundial.
- ☐ Make a ball size of a golf ball with your clay and place it at the center of your white paper plate.
- ☐ Place the paper plate on a level ground and stick the pencil into the clay.
- ☐ Using your compass find the geographic north and tilt the pencil toward the direction of the geographic north.
- ☐ Look at the shadow that the pencil/stick casts and mark it using the marker with the time you did the marking.
- ☐ Set your alarm every hour and mark the shadow on your sundial every hour until sunset or when you have at least six measurements.

Guide Questions:

- ☐ Why did the shadow cast by the pencil/stick keeps moving?
- ☐ Explain what is happening to the Earth as the shadow moves around the sundial.

Activity B: Life Cycle of a Star

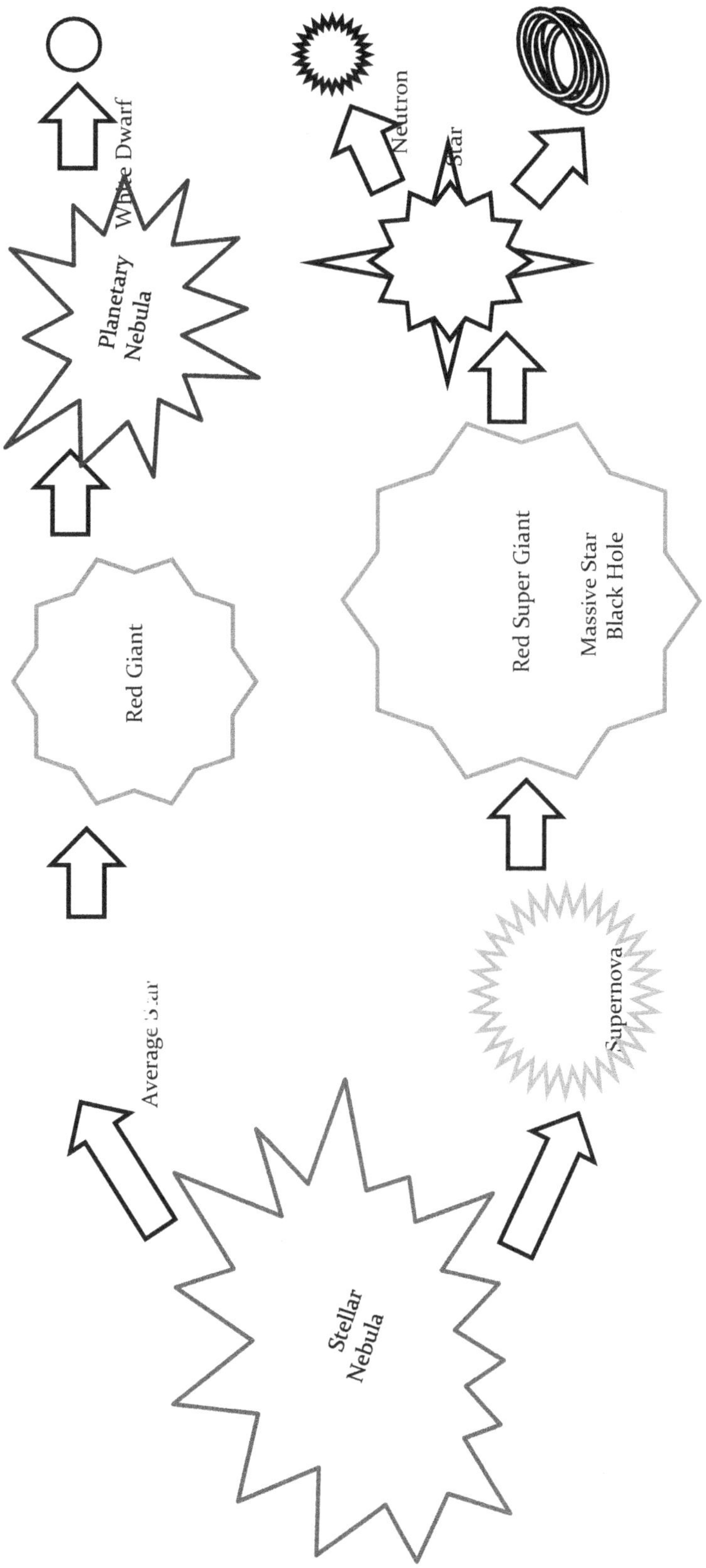

Activity C: Nature Journaling

First star spotted

First Hour

Second Hour

Third Hour

Unit 29: The Moon

- ☐ LESSON A: Observation and Discussion
  - Read the lesson carefully to make sure you have all needed supplies and you understand the content.
- ☐ ACTIVITY A: Focus on Vocabulary
  - Complete this hands-on activity with your student.
- ☐ ACTIVITY B: Focus on Vocabulary
  - Color the different stages in the life cycle of star.
  - Color the Stellar Nebula - Purple, Average Star - Yellow, Red Giant - Red, Planetary Nebula - Dark Blue and White Dwarf - White, Massive Star - Light Blue, Red Supergiant - Red Orange, Supernova - White, Neutron Star - Yellow and Black Hole - Black.
- ☐ ACTIVITY C: Nature Journaling
  - Look at the night sky for three days and observe the phases of the moon. Draw the moon inside the box and label your picture of what phase it is at.
- ☐ PARENT NOTES:

____

____

Lesson A: Features of the Surface of the Moon

Objective:

1) To observe how craters are created on the surface of the moon
2) To create a model of the different features of the surface of the moon.

Before the Lesson:

- Check the weather before the lesson and decide to conduct the lesson inside or outside.
- Gather materials for the activity.

Materials Needed:

For the demonstration:

- ☐ Plastic rectangular container (shoe box size) with flour three-quarters full
- ☐ 3-4 varying sizes and weight of rocks or balls
- ☐ Tape measure or meter stick

For the moon surface model:

- ☐ 1 circular rice cake for each student
- ☐ Crunchy peanut butter or Sunbutter (if have peanut allergy)
- ☐ Handful of Cheerios cereal per student
- ☐ Grape Jelly
- ☐ Crushed graham crackers
- ☐ Paper plates
- ☐ Knife to spread jelly and peanut butter

In-Class:

7. Class Observation:

☐ Invite the students to sit in a semicircle around you.

☐ Review the information learned in the previous lesson, specially how the moon orbits the Earth. Use the model the students created for Unit 27.

☐ Ask the students what they know about our moon.

- Do they know what it is made of? Can they student describe what the moon looks like?
- The students might describe the shape of the moon based on its different phases.

  Tell the students that they will learn about moon phase in another activity for the week.
- Tell the students that our moon is a natural satellite that orbits the Earth.

  You can read some facts about the moon and show pictures of the moon.
- Ask the students to describe what the surface of the moon looks like. Tell the students that only one side of the moon is seen from Earth. This side is called 'The Near Side'.

  Highlight some surface features using pictures.

  The Near Side has two features.

  1) *Mare/Maria- this is the dark parts of the moon previously thought as bodies of water hence the name Mare which means sea. These darker areas of the moon are low lying and are made of solidified lava(basalt) from previous lunar volcanic activities.*
  2) *Highlands- this part of The Near Side is lighter in appearance and higher in elevation. Possibly made from impact craters.*

  The other side of the moon that is unseen from Earth is called the 'Far Side'.

  The entire surface of the moon is covered with regolith and dotted with craters.

  3) *Craters- the craters vary in sizes up to as big as the Antarctica. These craters are believed to be formed when asteroids or comets hit the surface of the moon in very high velocity.*
  4) *Regolith- the layer on the moon surface made up fine dust and small rock fragments.*

8. Class Activity:

   A) Demonstration- Tell the students that the surface of the moon has many craters in varying sizes. Ask the students what could be the reason why these craters vary in depth and size?

   - Place the plastic container with flour and tell the students that the flour represents the surface of the moon.
   - Show the students <u>similar</u> size rocks or balls and tell them that these represent asteroids or comets in space. One ball/rock should be heavier than the other. Ask the students to predict which of the ball/rock will create a deeper crater if dropped at the same height.

- Drop the two balls/rocks with similar size but different mass at the same height from the surface of the flour. Observe.

  The heavier ball should create a deeper crater and displaced flour higher.

- Next, use two balls/rocks of different sizes. Ask the students which of the ball/rock will create a wider crater when dropped at the same height.

- Drop the two balls/rocks with different sizes at the same height from the surface of the flour. Observe.

  The bigger ball should create a wider crater.

- Try to drop all balls/rocks at the same time and observe the width and depth of the craters these different balls/rocks created.

- Extension: Drop the balls/rocks at varying heights and observe how the height where you drop them affect the width and depth of the crater the balls/rocks created.

B) Model of the moon surface- Tell the students that they will create an edible model of the surface of the moon.

- First distribute one rice cake per student.

- Tell the students that they will first create the Mare area of the moon using grape jelly. Have the students spread some grape jelly on one section of their rice cake.

- Next, have students cover the rest of their rice cake with peanut butter or sun butter.

- Ask the students to place some of their cheerios in a random pattern on the peanut butter/sun butter area to represent the craters on the moon surface.

- Then sprinkle some crushed graham crackers to represent the regolith (dust and rock fragments that cover most of the moon surface.

- Using the butter knife, make peaks with the peanut butter/ sun butter spread to show the highland part of the moon.

- Instruct the students to draw the model of the surface of the moon they created, showing the different features in the Observation Record 'Surface of the Moon.'

- Enjoy your moon surface treat!

9. Class Discussion:

   - Go over the result of the demonstration. Discuss how the size and mass of the asteroid/comet affects the size and depth of the crater.

The higher the mass of the asteroid or comet, the ______________________________ *the crater it creates.*

The bigger the asteroid or comet, the ____________________________________ *the crater it creates.*

a. How come the features of the surface of the moon remain the same for many years since the last asteroid bombardment? *The moon has no atmosphere (air/wind) to change its surface features.*

Activity A: Phases of the Moon

Using the information sheet below as a guide, cut and paste in the right position the different phases of the moon as it orbits around the Earth.

Optional: Instead of using the illustration provided, you can use chocolate cookies with white filling to demonstrate the different phases of the moon. Remove the white filling using butter knife to show the different moon phases.

Phases of the Moon as It Orbits Around Earth

Information sheet from
https://starchild.gsfc.nasa.gov/docs/StarChild/teachers/moonglow2.html

Materials Needed:

- ☐ Scissor
- ☐ Glue

*If using edible model

- ☐ 10-12 chocolate cookies with white filling
- ☐ Butter knife

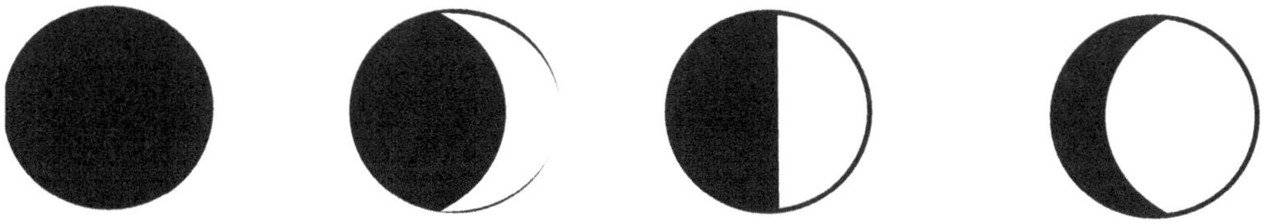

NEW MOON WAXING CRESCEN FIRST QUARTER WAXING
GIBBOUS

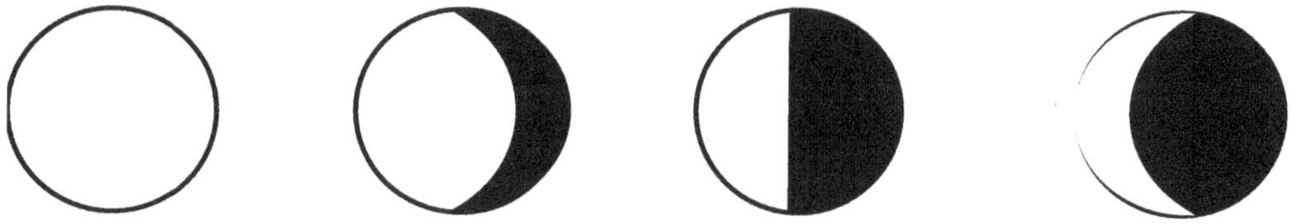

FULL MOON WANING GIBBOUS LAST QUARTER WANING
CRESCENT

☐

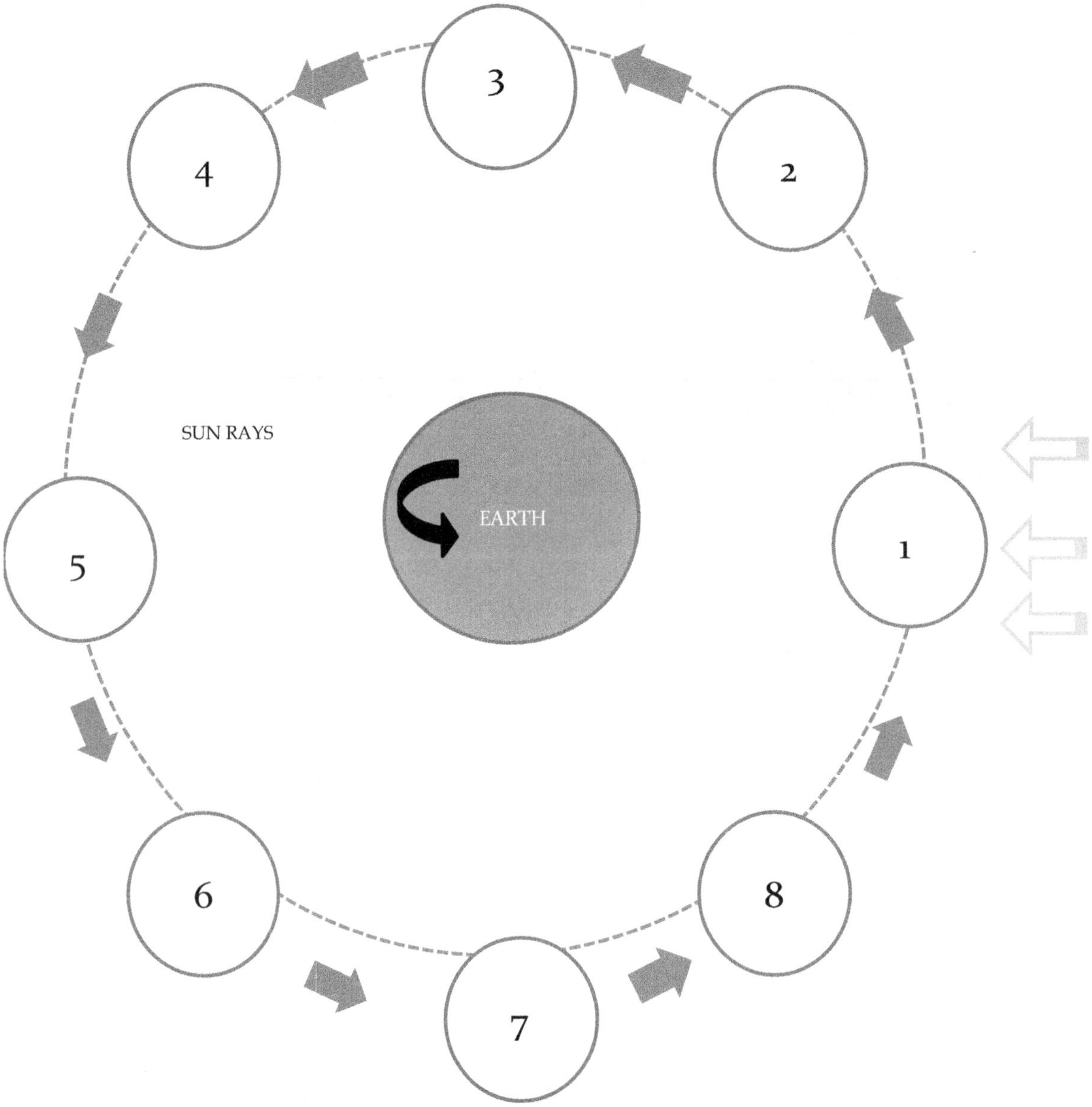
3
2
4
SUN RAYS
EARTH
1
5
6
8
7

Activity B: Moon Crater Add-Up Game

Materials:

- Two dice
- Copy of the 'Moon Crater Add-up' game card, one for each player
- Small rocks as markers for the game, eleven for each player

How to Play:

- Minimum of 2 players to play
- Each player needs a Game Card.
- The youngest player rolls the dice first then everyone takes turn counter-clockwise.
- Each player in their turn will roll two dice and add up the total number to mark their moon crater game card. For example, if the player rolls 2 and 4, he or she will place a rock on crater 6.
- Whoever fills up all of the eleven moon craters first, wins the game.

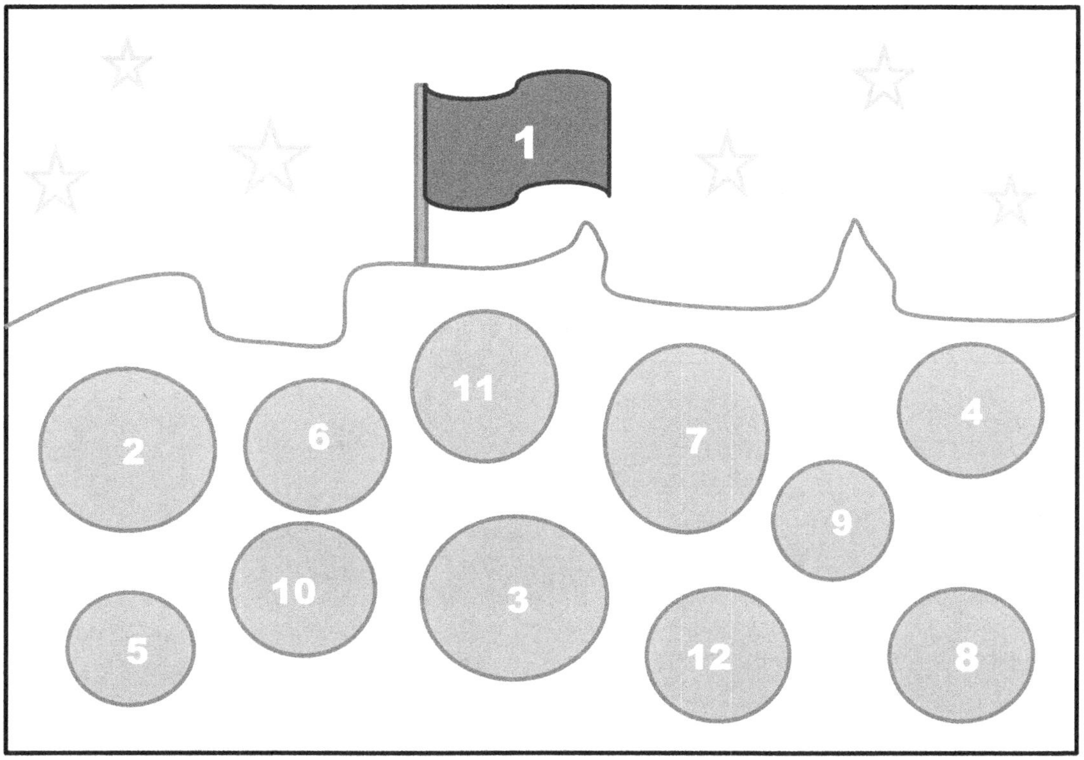

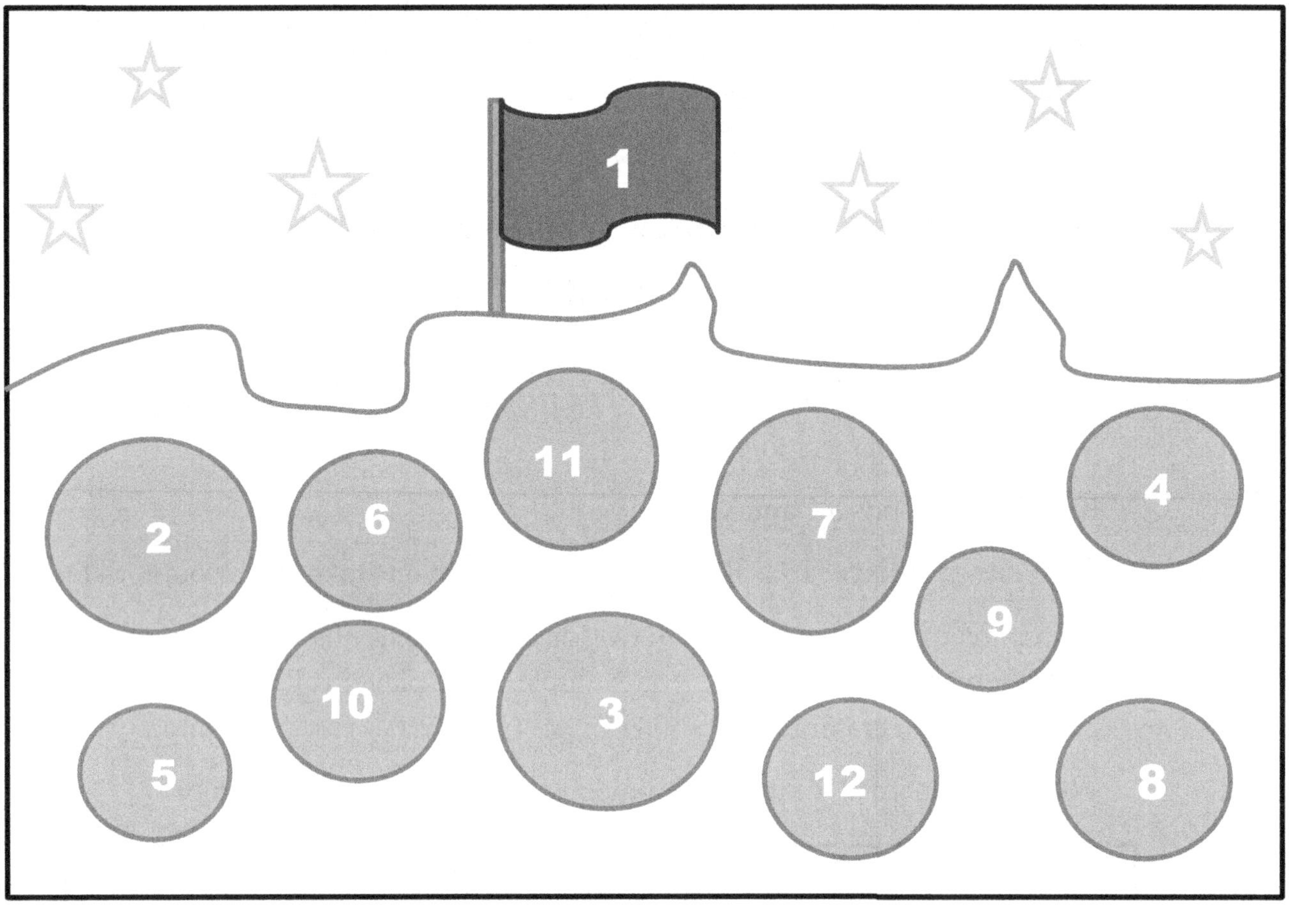
1
11
2
6
7
4
9
10
3
5
12
8

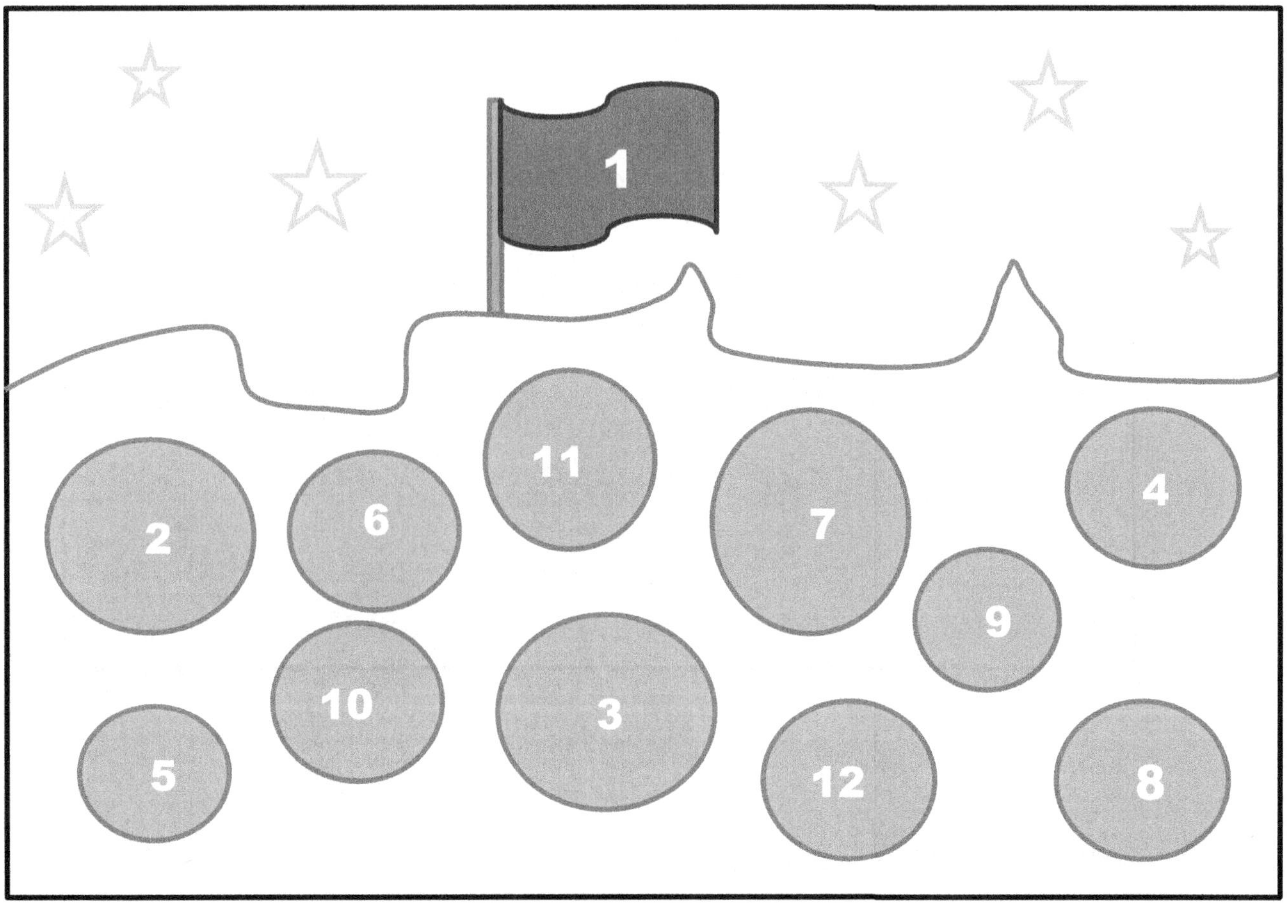
1
11
2
6
7
4
9
10
3
5
12
8

Activity C: Nature Journaling

Night 3

Night 2

Nigh 1

Unit 30: Patterns in the Sky

- ☐ LESSON A: Observation and Discussion
  - o Read the lesson carefully to make sure you have all needed supplies and you understand the content.
  - o Observation Record: Use the following pictures as a guide to learn about some of the most popular constellations.
- ☐ ACTIVITY A: Nature Journaling
  - o Using a star wheel, look at a night sky and find constellations that would be present at this time of the year. Draw the constellation/s you observed.
- ☐ ACTIVITY B: Focus on Vocabulary
  - o Copy and/or cut the following questions to make a Jeopardy Board.
  - o Arrange the papers based on CATEGORIES and POINTS.
- ☐ PARENT NOTES:

____

____

____

____

____

____

Lesson A: Patterns in the Sky

Objective:

1) To observe different patterns seen in the night sky.
2) To be familiar with the different constellations in the night sky.

Before the Lesson:

- Check the weather before the lesson and decide to conduct the lesson inside or outside.
- Gather materials for the activity.

Materials Needed:

- ☐ Observation Record 'Constellations'
- ☐ Mini marshmallows
- ☐ Bamboo sticks

In-Class:

1. Class Observation:

☐ Invite the students to sit in a semicircle around you.

☐ Review the information learned in the previous lesson, specially how the Earth orbits around the sun.

☐ Ask the students if they have tried to connect the stars in the sky and see pictures of animals and other objects.

☐ Tell the students that these 'pictures' that are made when you connect the stars with imaginary lines are called CONSTELLATION.

Constellations are groups or set of stars that when connected together using imaginary lines depict mythological characters, animals and objects.

There are 88 official known constellation that have been recognized by the International Astronomical Union (IAU).

Constellations helped ancient people to organize the night sky into a recognizable form which they used to predict the seasons, measure times and for directional or navigational purposes.

☐ Ask the students if they have seen or used a GPS (Global Positioning System) when they travel in cars? Before the invention of maps and GPS, what do you think early navigators use for direction? Have they heard about the North Star or Polaris?

The North Star or Polaris is a star that is always present in the Night Sky if you live in the Northern Hemisphere. This star marks the North Celestial Pole and helped early navigators to have a sense of what direction they are going.

2. Class Activity:

   . Explain to the students that for this activity, they will make model of different constellations using marshmallows and sticks.

   a. Give the students copies of the Observation Record 'Constellations'

   b. If time is limited you can assign a constellation to each student to make.

   c. Once everyone is done, ask the students to share the constellation they made and read some facts about them.

3. Class Discussion:

   . Ask the students if the constellation we see in the Northern Hemisphere is the same as what we can see in the Southern Hemisphere? Why or Why not?

   a. Would the constellation we see in the summer months similar or different than the constellations we see during the winter months? Why or Why not? Tie it in with the revolution of Earth around the Sun.

Observation Record: Constellation

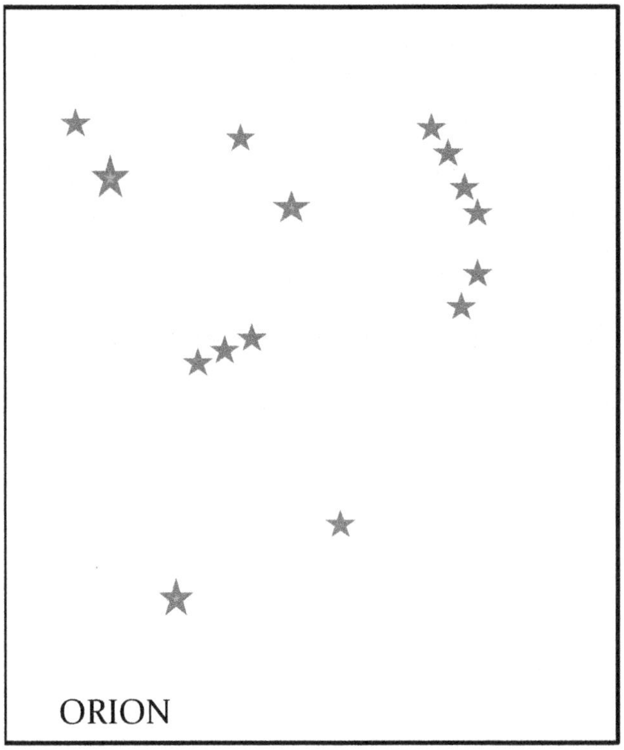

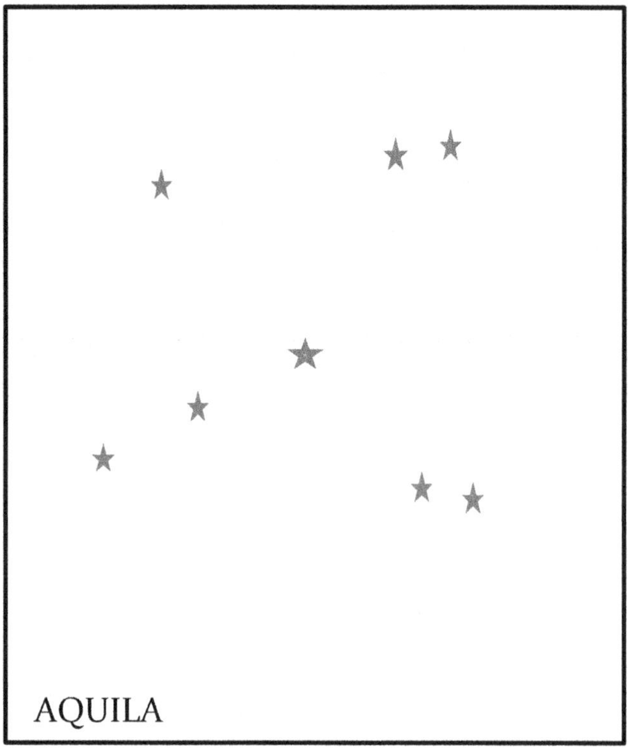

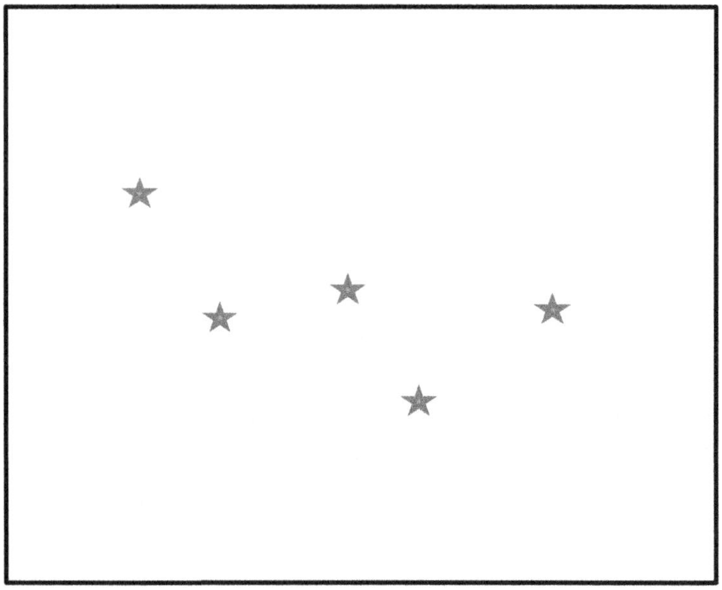

CANIS MAJOR

LEO

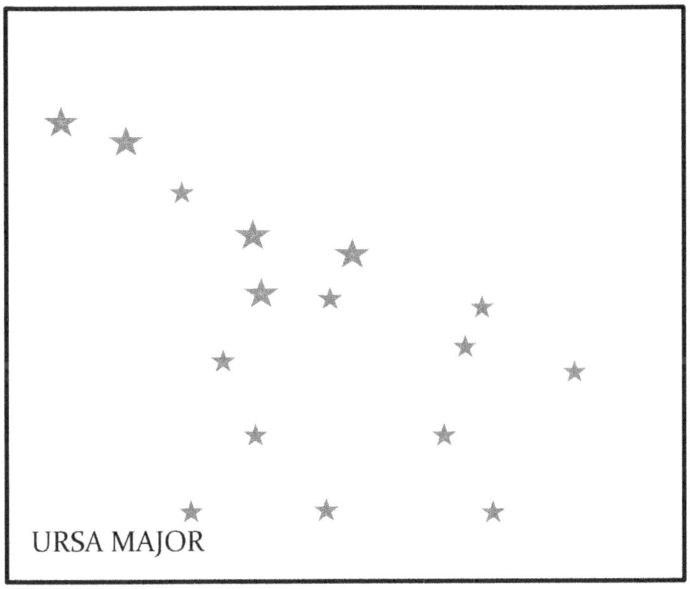
URSA MAJOR

LYRA

SCORPIUS

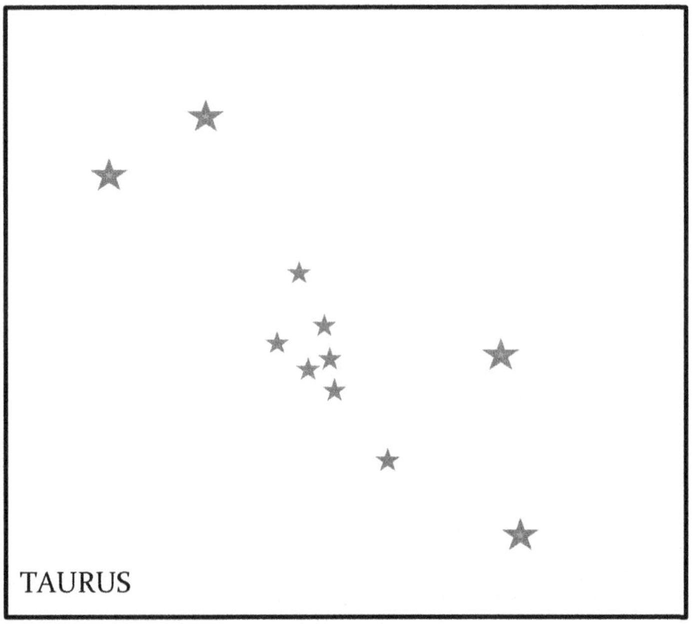
TAURUS

Activity A: Constellation

Materials Needed:

- ☐ Star Wheel (you can buy one or use this website to make your own https://www.skyandtelescope.com/astronomy-resources/make-a-star-wheel/)
- ☐ Scissors
- ☐ Stapler
- ☐ Writing material

____

(Name of Constellation)

Date ____

Location ____

Activity B: Astronomy Jeopardy Game

CATEGORY: Water Water Everywhere

100 Points This process turns liquid water to gas. Answer: What is EVAPORATION?	200 Points Rain, hail, sleet and snow are types of this part of the water cycle. Answer: What is PRECIPITATION?
300 Points Two of these atoms together with one Oxygen atom make up the water molecule. Answer: What are HYDROGEN ATOMS?	400 Points Most of the water absorbed by plants are released back in to the air through the small pores found under the leaves involving this process. Answer: What is TRANSPIRATION?

CATEGORY: How's the Weather Up There?

100 Points The average weather such as temperature and precipitation in a given area over a period of time, will give you this condition. Answer: What is CLIMATE?	200 Points This instrument measures the change in the atmospheric pressure. Answer: What is a BAROMETER?
300 Points A type of cloud that is found in high-altitude appears wispy, and made up of ice crystals. Answer: What is CIRRUS CLOUD?	400 Points The layer of the atmosphere which is the coolest and where meteor burns. Answer: What is the MESOSPHERE?

CATEGORY: In the Deep Blue Sea

100 Points The largest reservoir of water on Earth. Answer: What is the OCEAN?	200 Points These microscopic organisms are the primary producers in the marine environment and are found in the photic zone. . Answer: What are PHYTOPLANKTON?
300 Points No sunlight penetrates this depth. This zone is in total darkness. Answer: What is the BATHYPELAGIC or ABYSSAL ZONE	400 Points Some fish in the mesopelagic zone use this strategy where the coloration of their bottom part is lighter while the top part is darker. It is a form or camouflage Answer: What is COUNTERSHADING

CATEGORY: Heavenly Bodies

100 Points The center of our solar system and the closets star to our planet. Answer: What is the SUN?	200 Points The first four planets closest to the Sun is termed as this. . Answer: What are TERRESTRIAL PLANETS?
300 Points The group or set of stars that depicts mythological characters, animals or objects. Answer: What is CONSTELLATION	400 Points These are pieces of asteroids or comets that enter the Earth's atmosphere and survived the impact on Earth's surface. Answer: What are METEORITES?

CATEGORY: More Heavenly Bodies

100 Points Not the closest but the hottest planet in our solar system. Answer: What is VENUS?	200 Points Features on the surface of the moon caused by bombardment of asteroids and comets. Answer: What are CRATERS?
300 Points The phase of the moon shown here is called this.  Answer: What is WANING CRESCENT?	400 Points When a comet gets close to the Sun, parts of the nucleus outgas forming this part that surrounds the nucleus. Answer: What is the CORONA?

Made in the USA
Columbia, SC
18 August 2022

64861595R00150